I Saw What *NOT* to Do!

Chronicling a Life Journey of Triumph Over Circumstance

Dr. Charles W. Bridges III

Foreword by Mark J. Chironna, PhD

© Charles W. Bridges III Ed.D. All Rights Reserved

Divine Destiny Entertainment Group LLC.
Publishing Division (USA)
3255 S. John Young Parkway, Kissimmee. Florida. 34746 (USA)

Published by Divine Destiny Entertainment Group LLC Publishing Division.

First Printing, October 2014

1 1 1 1 1 1 9 0 6

Copyright © 2014 by Charles W. Bridges III EdD
All Rights Reserved.

The Divine Destiny Entertainment Group LLC name and logo are trademarks of the DDEG family of companies.

ISBN-13: 978-0-6-923-1098-4

Printed in the United States of America

LIBRARY OF CONGRESS CATOLOGING-IN- PUBLICATION APPLICATION IS FORTHCOMING

Without limiting the rights under the copyright reserved above, no part of this publication may be reproduced, stored in or introduced into a retrieval system, or transmitted, in any form, or by any means (electronic, mechanical, photocopying, recording, or otherwise), without the prior written permission of both the copyright owner and the above book publisher.

Although the author and publisher have made every effort to ensure that the information in this book was correct at press time, the author and publisher do not assume and hereby disclaim any liability to any party for any loss, damage, or disruption caused by errors or omissions, whether such errors or omissions result from negligence, accident, or any other cause.

You are equipped with the power to change your world!

Chapter Index

Chapter 1	The Bully	19
Chapter 2	Coming of Age	31
Chapter 3	Eliza	44
Chapter 4	"Pop"	55
Chapter 5	Which Way to Turn (Choices)	67
Chapter 6	Mr. Anderson (My Mentor)	78
Chapter 7	Is Church Everyday?	89
Chapter 8	Working Hard Versus Working Smart	101
Chapter 9	The Hustle	114
Chapter 10	Choosing to Be Different	126
Chapter 11	"Faith, Patience and Trust"	136
Chapter 12	Bishop Carlton Pearson	146
Chapter 13	Mental Toughness	157
Chapter 14	The Process	165
Chapter 15	The Imaginative Mind	177
Chapter 16	Finding a Way to Win	186
Chapter 17	What *Not* to Do!	195
'Lifeisms'		208

Don't Just Take My Word for It

I Saw What *NOT* to Do is a book that embodies timeless principles without preaching. As we go on a life journey with Dr. Bridges, he shares powerful 'life-ism's' that if applied, can change our lives. This is a must-read for all ages!

Glenn Carson
Entrepreneur

Charles has always been an engaging, passionate and motivational speaker. He has now translated this passion and energy into writing his first publication a personal development manual. Enjoy!!!

Adam Judd
North America Sourcing Director
KONE Inc.

I strongly agree with Charles in that, "we shape our future with the choices of today." It is important for people to remember that success in academics, martial arts, and every other task requires work on your attitude and strong, continuous effort.

Master Namsoo Hyong
President of MD TKD Association
USA Delegate for WoMAU

This book is dedicated to my family: To my beautiful and courageous wife Nicole and my three wonderful children Nickolas, Jaz, and Brooke.

Success principles don't change but we must.

Preface

There are volumes of bibliographies on presidents of nations, heads of states, world leaders and people of prominence in our society. There are stories that we call stories of "rags to riches", stories of people who have found a way to reach achievements the naysayers said were impossible. There are countless tales that have been written, but no one can tell a story like the person who has lived it. To read a story about a warrior who has seen great triumph and has borne the pain of great defeat, challenges those who read the words to try and understand what that soldier endured.

As you read this story think about your neighborhood and how were you raised. What did your parents do for a living? Think about how your parents' occupations influenced what you wanted to do when you grew up. Think about these things because so often we are not aware of how connected we are to the world around us. Sometimes this interconnection to our environment can be fruitful and beneficial, and other times it may hold us back from reaching our full potential.

This is my story, and there is no one who can tell it better. This story is about me, but it's *for* you. It's for those struggling with personal identity, those who are not sure that they can accomplish the dreams and the goals they have on the inside. This story is also for people who are already successful but want to gain a new perspective in finding added prosperity. This story is for anyone, because it's about real life, not a Hollywood portrayal of what happens in the real world. This story is about winning despite the odds: this story is about finding your inner voice, the inner voice that some may call it the Holy Ghost, some may call it Allah, Buddha, Brahma, or Yahweh. Still others use terms such as intuition, gut feelings or instincts to identify this inward guidance we all possess. Finding this voice no matter what you call it, and understanding that this voice is one of the keys to your personal triumph is essential to your success.

Let me also address the use of the word success. First of all, when I use the word success, what I am really referring to is prosperity. Dictionary.com says that prosperity is a successful, flourishing, or thriving condition, especially in financial respects; good fortune. Prosperity denotes a more wholesome, balanced, and sustainable idea of abundance. I use the term success throughout the book in order to keep things simple, as success is a more readily identifiable term. Merriam Webster's dictionary says that there are several definitions of success. Some of these definitions are: an outcome or result, a favorable or desired outcome, or the attainment of wealth, favor or eminence. Eminence according to Webster's dictionary is the condition of being well known and successful, a person of high rank, or an area of high ground or elevation.

Based on the definition of success, one could infer that success is related to being well known or simply achieving a desired result. In other words, success means several different things, and we can individually determine what it means for ourselves. So as you read this story if you have already determined what success is to you -fantastic, if not, here is an opportunity to define what success means to you. The beautiful thing is that this is what it means to be an individual, and this is one of many choices we have.

Although this story is about my personal journey towards success, I understand my success is incomplete without benefiting someone else; therefore, this story is for your benefit. It was written so that you will understand that you were created for a purpose, and so you will know without a doubt that you can *"triumph over your circumstance"*. The next time you ask someone how they're doing and they say "under the circumstances, fairly well", after you read this book you will wonder what are they doing under there?

While I am talking about success, let me also provide a warning to those of you afraid of achieving greatness in your life. If you are uncomfortable with the idea that you may escape a normal and comfortable level of living and enter a new dimension of awareness and triumph, this book is *not* for you. This book is not for the person who desires to live a "normal life." The information here can cause you to achieve beyond what your friends, neighbors, or relatives have ever dreamed of. To be clear, I am not just talking about money, because I know that's what most think about. I am talking about a heightened level of self-awareness, a new perspective, a larger concept of confidence and belief in your self.

I am talking about money as well, because I firmly believe that as we become better, and do better, our new way of life attracts new levels of living that include financial success. So do not continue reading if you enjoy average relationships, average imagination, average creative ability or average bank accounts. Read on if your desire is to see what NOT to do.

Above all this story is about looking at the choices and actions that others make in their lives and critically thinking about those choices and resulting outcomes. If you haven't figured it out as of yet, in nearly every aspect of our lives, the outcomes generally have the greatest level of significance. To think about the behavior and choices of others from the perspective of what you can see that they did well, and what you can see that they could improve upon, provides a new pathway to personal development. Or if you are like me, and you have things surrounding you that you really do not want in your life, I sincerely hope this book will help you identify a new perspective on these things.

My goal in writing this book ultimately, is to aid the reader in developing a mindset that allows them to see what others are doing wrong, and decide not to do those same things.

I am convinced this life is a 'thinking woman's game' (a thinking man's game as well). I also have learned that our mindset and perspective often times determines our results and outcomes. When I reflect on my personal development, I think about the fact that I learned to see the mistakes in others actions and decisions when I was young. I discovered this insight was a success principle for me, and one that helped shape my life.

Perhaps those beyond the teenage years in their 20s or 30s, may think this principle is one that doesn't apply to them. I must disagree. If you can learn from the mistakes of others, you can benefit from this knowledge and apply the principles I outline in this book at any age. From my experience, once you uncover the ability to see how things can be much more fruitful by changing your actions learning from the mistakes others make, you can construct dramatic improvements in many areas of your life.

Many of us, were not born with a "silver spoon" in our mouths. Many of you reading this book grew up poor and had little direction when you were young. Others of you had single parent households that caused emptiness and feelings of abandonment, and rejection.

Still others of you were raised in good families, perhaps middle class families with plenty of money and social status, but you still lacked the positive support, or direction or whatever it was that was missing that ails you today. Let's face it - we all have things we can improve on, right? Well, one of the things that I have found brings success, is looking at other people's successes and failures and applying what works and not applying what doesn't work to our own lives. It seems so simple right? It is. It is a simple concept, there is much work to be done to achieve the success we all desire, but the master plan is already in place.

    Today we have a nation that has never been more polarized and divided on so many issues and perspectives. While I encourage individuality, I simultaneously promote unity. Therefore, this story is not about making us see the differences in one another.
This story is about the importance of the inner power that we each have. No matter your religious affiliation, no matter the values that you hold dear to your heart, you are a soul. You are someone's child; you are likely someone's brother or someone's sister, and if not, at some level you are connected to someone else. You have a brain, a body, you have clothes, and you are a human being.

We are all connected, and whether we like it or not, everything that we do can potentially impact those around us. Why is this important? It's important because as we learn to embrace the identity we have, who we are, we can better serve those around us. As you learn and develop the winner, the champion the survivor inside you, this book's goal is to provide a spark and a desire to help you do the same. There are always those that I call the "dream killers". These are the people who act as if they are your friends; they act as if they have your best interest at heart.

This is their weapon, their disguise is to appear as though they are for you, but secretly they seek to destroy you. As a young man I witnessed an environment that was not conducive to the production of positive outcomes and have seen what dream killers can do to people, organizations, and corporations. If there is one lesson that I have learned that perhaps could enrich you, the person reading these pages, is to have and defend fiercely a foundational set of core values.

My family did not have a set of values that was at the core of who they were. As I grew up, all I knew was that going to church is what you were supposed to do, and God was a good God.

Of course, there were many more lessons than those in church. My point however, is that my family did not instill a set of principles that were plain and simple. My family was teaching me things, but I had to discover the principles myself. This journey called life is about growing, changing, and developing an inner character that is grounded on foundational principles that cause a person to stand through adversity.

Things surrounding these principles change, but the principles and values remain constant. The question is, will you change because the world around you says what you believe in is not right?

In case you have never looked up the definition of the word principle, Merriam Webster says a principle is a fundamental law, doctrine, or truth that explains how or why something works. It has always been important to me to think about why I am doing what I am doing. I have often thought- is this behavior, task or work that I am engaged in going to produce a positive result? In time I discovered that there are principles that often govern the outcomes we receive, and most often they are derived from biblical principles.

Throughout these writings I discuss religion, the universe and the energy we all possess. These are my beliefs, some things that I discuss from my perspective can be supported scientifically, others items cannot. Either way, this story is a depiction of a very challenged beginning that through application of the principles I discuss has resulted in prosperity.

In this book, I talk about my life, how I was raised, the choices I made, the mistakes I made, but interwoven in the fabric of my life story, is my character development. This is where the lessons are, how to overcome things that are seemingly insurmountable, how to keep going when there seems to be no fuel left in the tank, this is what I want you to take away from this book. So, as you read about my life, please keep in mind that there are stories within the stories, and from time to time, I will hop up on my soapbox and tell you what I think is the best way to address certain issues that come against us all. I have developed what I call "Lifeisms". I have a "Lifeism" above the title of each chapter simply because I think they are a source of inspiration and I hope the "Lifeisms" will make you think.

Webster's dictionary says that an "ism" is a belief, attitude, or distinctive doctrine. You might think of the term capitalism to help you understand why I chose to add the "ism" to life.

So my "Lifeisms" are lessons that I've learned, often times these beliefs came from people that were smarter than me. Please know it is a good thing to surround yourself with and learn from people smarter than you.

Let me give you the first Lifeism# 1 **_When speaking to someone who has something you want in life, shut up and listen!_** Sorry to put it so bluntly but we were designed with more airways to gain information than to give information for a reason. That is to say, for those that don't get it right away, we have two ears and one mouth for a specific purpose!

I have included areas wherein you may write notes I hope you will find this is helpful. I remember reading several books and I would have a great thought that would come to me as I was reading but I didn't have a place to write about it, the notes section is for those ideas that you feel are relevant to your development.

I have had several life coaches, people that may not have known they were coaching me, but their knowledge and influence was helping me to shape my character and my personal development. I hope that some of the examples, principles and what I call 'Lifeisms' help you to become a better you and help you see what _**Not**_ to Do!!

Foreword

"Our journey in life is one that is filled with challenges as well as opportunities. Learning how to navigate our path in faith while discovering the ways of the Spirit and being led by the Spirit to wholeness and well being finds us living on the edge of genuine adventure. While the path is at times unorthodox and often unpredictable, our responses to it determine the outcomes we obtain. Dr. Bridges is offering you a window into his own journey. Allow his heart to touch your heart and his insights along the way to add value to your own personal journey, you will be enlarged by it all."

Bishop Mark J. Chironna, MA, PhD
Church On The Living Edge
Orlando, Florida

The moment you begin to understand that the world doesn't revolve around you, your perspective is prepared for success.

Chapter 1: The bully

All I can remember is that when I woke up that morning, I didn't want to go to school. I didn't have a bad dream so that was good; sometimes my dreams were about my dying, what is that about? At times I thought, am I going to die when I am young? Well anyway, the fifth grade was a big deal. One of the first things that came to mind that morning was I had to be careful around white people. Although I saw white people around my neighborhood, it seemed like there were problems that existed between black people and white people. My older sisters were always trying to look out for me, but as I remember it they only played with black kids and I didn't' understand that. I was cool with whomever, I liked the white kids, the black kids, the asian kids in fact all the young people in my neighborhood were all right. It was just that even though I thought all the kids were pretty cool I didn't want to get my feelings hurt.

I like Ricky, Ricky is white, and I don't know what was in that cigarette he gave me last week, but my head seemed like it was moving in circles but my feet didn't move.

Ricky's little sister Melanie thinks I'm cute, but I am only 10 years old and she is 14. Rick is twenty-two and I know that he said he is going to the military and he doesn't like to listen to his mom. He is always fighting with his mom and calling her names, yelling at her and stuff. Man my mom would knock me down the flight of stairs in our apartment if I talked to her like Ricky talked to his mom. The other day when I was getting of the school bus I saw Ricky yelling at his mom, He said "Who in the hell do you think you are talking to, you don't run S#@*, the only reason I still live here is because I don't leave for basic training yet, you make me sick".

    He slammed the door and spit on it. (OK, let's be clear, this is a family friendly book, but this is what he said, I'm just saying). I thought Ricky needed to take some medicine or something; he had a bad attitude with his mom. "Junior" (my nickname back then) get down those stair' it's time to eat and get on the bus. My dad was calling me.

    Ah, man, I am still in the bed. I must have drifted back off to sleep, so I was dreaming about all that stuff, wow that's too funny. O.k. so the fifth grade is going to be cool. I can do this; I knew that riding the bus was going to be a problem.

The older kids on the bus were going to be talking junk and I don't want to fight anybody. My two older sisters are always hogging the bathroom. (BOOM BOOM-BOOM) as I bang on the door, Denise gets out the bathroom and tries to kiss me, I'm like please back up off the sexy. Michelle was already dressed; this chick is practicing the trumpet at 7:30 am in the morning. Michelle is sort of nerdy if you ask me, she seems like she is always reading.

I love my sisters, they are the best, they think they run this, but they don't run a thing. Deep down they know that if Mom is on that rampage, they call me, "who you gonna call" Junior. Ah, that's funny, OK now somehow my morning is moving very quickly I am already on the bus, and it seems like a few minutes ago I was in the bathroom. Everyone knows how mean school-age kids are, but the thing is as a 10-year-old boy, when you give other kids that are the same age as you something to laugh about, its just like adding fuel to a hot burning flame. My mother put about six ounces of Vaseline on my face because she said it helped to protect your skin. December in Illinois is no joke.

The weather here gets so cold, if you pee in the snow, which I have done by the way, two words; awe-some, the pee turns into a yellow popsicle in ten seconds. I said a yellow Popsicle; I didn't say an edible one (that's funny). Why is everybody staring at me on this school bus? Oh yeah, half a pound of Vaseline, duh? You have to love your mom though. So I have big lips, and I know they are sexy, but the haters will hate. I hear the jokes, "Junior, it looks like your lips been filled up with a bicycle pump" one boy exclaims. "Dude did your lips get sucked into a vacuum?" another one yells.

Whatever, I'm moving on. It seemed were like there were a million acres of corn in my town, and if you lived in the country there is always that "farm smell". All my country people know that smell; it's like a blend of all the animals mixed with manure, Ewww. I wonder if farmers make money? They have to make money, they are always growing stuff. My school was Edison Middle School, and the school is pretty "tight" (organized, well kept). There were a lot of cute girls, they wanted me, I knew it and they did too. Soooo, fifth grade math, no joke, but I got this.

Sorry if you noticed I am not staying with one topic, I may bounce around a bit, but I am only 10 years old. There was a boy in my class named Joshua, Joshua and I were pretty cool, but he didn't have game like me. White boys do not have game. (To all my white readers out there, we already know there are certain things that many of you struggle with, like rhythm, clapping on beat, and "having game"). Oh yeah, "having game," means, the ability to intelligently hold a conversation with the opposite sex, so they start to like you.

From time to time I will interpret street language, but don't expect me to bail you out every time. Back to Joshua, every now and again, I was mean to other people and Joshua was an easy target. He was that guy with saggy pants, a goofy look and he was just kind of a punk. I thought to myself "one day I am going to mess with this dude". Then I thought, "today is that day, just 'cause I am bored and I want to mix it up". I didn't consider myself a bad bully. I was the kind of *cat* (guy) that just said what I thought, and I really didn't care whether it was polite or not. I was a little shorter than most people in my class, and I guess I had that short man's complex, or was it short boy's complex?

Either way I remember walking down the hall and I had to pee really bad and as I walked in the bathroom; guess who was in there? Joshua, and he was going pee in *my* usual stall. Now you know what is about to happen. "Joshua, get the h%$# off my stall man, you know that's where I pee every day punk" "Charles, (Joshua couldn't call me junior-he was not that cool) dude I know you see me peeing" SSSSSSSSSPOOOW, that was the sound my hand made when I smacked Joshua upside is face. I smacked this boy so hard that I remember seeing that slow motion action, like in transformers, and his face just turned bright pink, red and it was just pure joy to watch him scream. "AAAAAAHHHH", he yelled. He started crying, and I started punching, kicking and hitting him anywhere I could.

    The next thing I knew a teacher was grabbing me asking me what happened "He was going pee in my stall, I said". The next thing I knew I was in the principal's office, and the principal is on the phone with my mother. My mom was crazy, she would knock me out, so I really had to pee then, because I never went and now I was scared, scared for real of Momma Bridges.

I thought to myself, "I don't know what it was about hurting people that felt so good, but hopefully I will grow out of this stage, but right now, I am a bully and I like it". There were times when I was walking down the hall at Edison Middle School and would see someone else in the hallway, and I'd think to myself, "I wonder what it would feel like to smack them upside their head". What can I say, I am being honest, and that is what I was thinking about. It was time to go home, and I was happy because I wasn't enjoying school that day any way, I should have skipped. In case you are wondering about what my mom did to me, it was physical and it involved me screaming, yeah, she whipped my behind, but on with the story.

My grandfather was the coolest dude on the planet. One day he told me, "Life is so much sweeter if you stay off dem drugs, boy" (Grandpa was from Mississippi). I believed him, so I never messed with all that drug stuff. But is alcohol a drug? I didn't think it was, even if it was I wanted a drink that day. Now remember it was November in Illinois and cold is not the word, it was beyond cold. I was walking down Neil Street on a Saturday and I was thinking I should have put on more socks, "d@#! Its cold out here", I said to myself.

I get into the convenience store, and I see the alcohol section, and I knew I was about to steal something. I was broke, I had no money, and even if I did have money, I wanted to try and steal something anyway, just to see if I could get away with it. I saw this bottle of Reunite' peach (wine). Man my mouth was watering, so I took it. I saw the clerk step in the back, and I was out the door. That was the beauty of a winter coat, I thought to myself, "You got skills, boy".

My next thought was, "The only way I could enjoy this wine was to stay outside somewhere to drink it, so I wouldn't get caught by anyone. When I got to the park and nobody was around, it was time for my drink. The top on this bottle didn't want to come off, but I got it off and threw it back. Man, it felt, like my body was heating up, and my throat felt like it was getting a liquid massage. I said to myself, "I need to drink everyday".

This was my first time drinking, my parents were both ministers, they would kill me if they knew I was drinking. During this phase of my life, I was all about rebellion; completely engrossed in thinking of ways I could avoid complying with the systematic oversimplification that I saw in the lives of my parents and others around me.

I don't remember other times when I went crazy on someone as I did with Joshua in the fifth grade, but I know I had a bad attitude back then. Not only did I want to bully people and see how far I could push the limit on misbehaving, I wanted to be free of the restrictions being placed on me within my environment. Whether the restrictions came from my parents, religious ideals, or any source of authority, I wanted no part of it. I felt that I wanted to be destructive because I was expected to behave and be productive.

Perhaps this is providing some insight in to the "preacher kid" personalities some parents are dealing with. Or maybe you are a parent of a young person who is not making good choices, in several areas of their lives. I don't have the "silver bullet" solution but for me, I wanted to discard any elements of the influences of others.

I also wanted to disregard the rules, so perhaps this is what your child is experiencing. I am not a psychologist, nor do I understand the science behind all behaviors, but from my perspective, during this phase of my life it wasn't about being good, it was about just the opposite.

Later, I will talk about my grandmother and how she cared for me.

Some of the things that helped me to survive this dark period of my life were granny' prayers. Don't ask me how I know, but I know that her prayers helped me to redirect my life. Years after this period of my life had passed, my mother told me that during this time my grandmother was always praying for me, and I am so grateful that she did. Those prayers were the foundation of my new direction in life. As a result of my grandmother's love and support, along with my mother and other family members, my life changed course away from evils that can beset us all. Today, I am forever grateful for those prayers, and I see I now have the ability to help others along their journey.

As I reflect on this period of my life, I wonder how many other people that are reading this book were bullies or thieves in their younger years as I was and never got back on track. Perhaps you were a product of a single-parent home, and you didn't have the affirmation of a father's love. Or even worse, you were bullied, picked on, and ridiculed in your younger days. Maybe your parents fought constantly and you witnessed domestic violence.

Your home environment could have been similar to mine in that I had a relatively "normal" upbringing, but I still felt like I needed to rebel against the system.

If you are trying to gain insight into finding the right track, whatever the "right track" means to you, I would ask you to do the following. When you have the time, get yourself to a quiet place where you have no distractions. When I say no distractions, what you are trying to accomplish here is meditation, children or a husband or wife, or partner constantly interrupting your flow is not a good thing. Once you are alone, remember to bring a pencil and paper with you.

Take as long as you need. Remember the actual amount of time will vary amongst individuals, but if you desire to be fully in the moment, get a candle to have the room really dark to concentrate. Do whatever it takes to clear your mind. Do whatever it is required to have a peaceful environment. Close your eyes, and just let the world around you fade away. Spend this time allowing your inner voice speak to you, and write down what comes to you. I have done this for years, and this is one of the reasons I am writing this book.

This book came out of a period of time when I felt within my heart that my words would make a difference in people's lives. While I believe making a difference is essential, I also understand the importance of establishing myself as someone that people can rely on for relevant wisdom.

What holds you back today looks insignificant tomorrow once you've conquered the fear to start!

Chapter 2: Coming of Age

Edison Middle School, is the where, seventh grade is the when, you better know who's the who, and the how is how I came to posses the many skills I had with the ladies, Well, let's just say I had it like that. Is it a fair statement to say nearly every boy between the ages of 10 and 14 starts to think about girls? Well, maybe there were some boys who liked other boys, but this isn't about all that. I can remember that I wanted to impress as many girls as possible so, how do you do that? Sports.

First up is wrestling. So I was probably 4 feet 5 inches tall and not more than 100 pounds in the sixth grade, and I have never wrestled before. I was a black kid, and as far as I knew, black people didn't wrestle. Well, black folks in my family didn't wrestle, but it wasn't about that either. Yeah that's right it was all about the girls. Our school colors were red and white and I remember the first day I went into the gym. It's been a long time since I was in middle school, but all I remember is this room smelled like underwear.

So you know it had to be about the girls –why else would I have worn tights? Despite how I felt, you already know I *was* wearing the tights. I remember practicing with boys that were mostly bigger than me, and getting my butt whipped. I remember one time, this boy pinned me down so hard I felt like my spleen was going to pop open. I didn't know what the spleen does, but God put it there for a reason, I like my spleen. Wrestling lasted about 3 months, and that was a wrap.

Next up cross-country. Now, this was a little more like it. Don't go stereotyping me, not all African Americans run like those brothers from Kenya and Jamaica and places like that. Even though I know some countries in Africa are developed nations, I still get a visual of some lion chasing after a brother. This is just an example of too much influence from Television. Anyway, like I was saying cross-country was more like it, because I could run. I couldn't do a lot of things, but I could run. I could outrun just about anybody in my class. You have to be able to run when you mess with people like I did, I was always starting some sort of trouble.

When I needed to leave the scene of the crime, I put on the afterburners, and jetted. Some of you reading this remember when kids used to say "jet", ah back in the day. So, as I was saying, most kids who challenged me to a race lost, because I was small, but I had " the short man's complex" (An emotional impulse to over compensate in some form due to being short). I had something to prove, and a lot of times the girls would watch.

You know basketball was in the picture. This is a sport that black people can play, now come on, you have to admit that. If you grew up in the city, you probably don't know what square dancing is. Let me do the best I can to tell you about it. Square dancing to me was, simply put, what the cowboys did for fun. I am not a cowboy but this is how I saw it. Basically, there is country music, a lack of rhythm and a lot of yee-haw. If I remember correctly, I believe this was our P.E (physical education) class. (I must digress for a moment here. What is up with our schools today? Do we still have P.E? Do kids still play outside all day after school? I have the solution for all the childhood obesity we as a nation are dealing with-stop feeding the children in America junk, and make THE PLAY after school.

Making sure our children get their homework done is mandatory, and as an educator I understand the importance of this. However, if you are a parent and you are feeding your child unhealthy foods and not giving them playtime, shame on you.) Hopefully, I can get back to square dancing without feeling the need to step up on my soapbox. Sometimes the things we struggle with as a community seems so easy to fix, but the world tries to complicate them. As I was saying square dancing, did I say that this was both boring and awkward?

Can you imagine a black kid, trying to dance around to country music, saying yee-haw? Well, it was a mandatory part of P.E class so I did it. I remember the song would say something like "grab yer partner by the hand, and do that dance, yes you can". The way you did it was from time to time you would hook your arm through your partner's arm that was bent, and you would twirl around in a circle. Sometimes the whole class would get in a huge circle and twirl around. I am not 'hating' on my *country/cowboy* brothers and sisters, but it was not cool to square dance, at least not for the majority of people in my school.

However, there were girls there, all kinds of girls, and don't forget I liked girls.

As much as I hated square dancing, and I resented the fact that I had to wear those ridiculous tights for wrestling, during this period of life, I was learning about myself. One thing I found during this time is that as much as I wanted to be cool and hang with the cute girls, I wanted to learn. I wanted to learn, and as I began to learn about life, I learned about the importance of an education and the importance of thinking for myself.

This is one of those difficult topics to actually explain how it happened, but it just happened. I remember times when I was walking in the hallways of Edison and just thinking about the difference between what I thought about something and what a friend or a teacher thought about it. I couldn't give you specific examples, but I now see that if you want to develop a confident inner self at some point, you have to come to trust yourself, and have faith in the inner you.

As I am writing this, I am reflecting on school and how a young person's world begins to take shape as a result of the things that happen in their life.

Middle school is the beginning of the process of discovery for us. Young men and women are in the age range of puberty, and the pressures and influences of things outside the instructions from home begin to affect the direction life takes us all. During this time one thing I noticed is that there were not many positive male images in school or really in my life at all. I was fortunate in that my father was in my life, and he was able to shape my thinking and provide a positive masculine identity for me.

However, I remember that there were mostly all female teachers in my school. There were a few male teachers, but now that I think about it the men were not very visible, in my community. This may be a bit of regression from the conversation of how middle school began to create certain ideas about the world in my life, but take a moment and reflect on how the male perspective functioned in your life. Were both your parents in your home? Do you have positive images of men in your community? Do you have negative memories of your father, uncles, or male cousins?

Why is this important to discuss now, you may ask? As I said earlier I am discussing the age ranges of between 10 and 14 years, one of the most critical times in a young person's life.

It is my understanding that in certain cultures, such as Jewish communities, the age of accountability is 13 for boys and 12 for girls. As I understand it, at the Bar Mitzvah events for boys and Bat Mitzvah for girls, older Jews welcome young boys and girls into the community and recognize that these young people now have a greater level of responsibility and accountability. The young people are expected to participate in issues within the community at a greater level, including a deeper devotion to issues of religion, accountability, education and responsibility.

My point here is that I think it is noteworthy that attention to cultures such as Jewish societies is of particular importance. Many have observed that Jewish people have prospered, and as I reflect on conversations I have had with Americans about Jews I must say these conversations tend to discuss admiration for the way in which Jews handle many issues.

What else can be said about middle school? Well let me take this opportunity to speak to the preteens, teenagers, or parents of teenagers. I wrote this book for several reasons, one of which was to provide a dialogue regarding many of the issues people face today.

Perhaps you are in a middle-class family and are not struggling with many issues. Or maybe you and your family have identified or will identify with the challenges and difficulties set forth in this book. In either case, let me tell you how important loving your family and those within your community is. When I was writing this book, I reflected and thought about my middle school years, and through every night I cried on my pillow.

Through every meal I sat down to with very little on the plate, through every day I felt lonely, afraid, empty, confused, and every other emotion teenagers feel, my family was there. Many friends and relatives were there as well, so remember the simple fact of the matter is that you may not be "happy" with where you are now, but know within your gut and mind, it can change. That is to say, remain steadfast mentally towards a decision to change your life, but all the while love your family and loved ones, and watch how this love can help you through life's greatest battles.

Speaking of battles, I recall a situation where the love of my family, pulled me through a dark, dark time.

I can't remember how old I was exactly I just remember it was somewhere between the ages of 10 and 15. My neighborhood had gotten pretty bad with the drugs; the violence, and the murder rate had risen. I recall getting off the bus and being nervous just walking a block or so to my grandmother's house. My family moved in with my grandparents for a short while, and during this time I saw how a negative environment and troubled community could impact one's life. During one summer a few people I knew where shot, one or two people were killed and one murder was just on the other side of town. The word on the street was that the person who was shot had lost five dollars in a card game and got upset, and ended up dead. This really scared me, because I knew the exact apartments where he was murdered in I rode my bike in that area all the time.

  These shootings and deaths were bad but that same summer one incident just pushed me over the edge mentally. One day I was shooting baskets at King Park up the street from my house and everything was cool. I didn't have any beef with anybody in the park and we did not see any gang members, so it was all-good.

It was just another day when I saw a scuffle or maybe even a few blows get thrown on the basketball court - this was just the neighborhood. About two hours into game time, a couple cars pulled onto the court. I didn't know the guys but they were older and looked like trouble. When they first arrived they seemed cool. They popped the trunk of their cars just to play music, not to cause any trouble. At least that's what I thought.

    The whole time these guys where there, it was a set up. They were looking for someone. The guy they were looking for was in the pickup basketball game that I was playing in. The next thing I knew somebody yelled something like "Dude, get your stuff away from here"!! I saw one of the guys whose car was on the court reach into his trunk, grab a pistol and head straight towards me. He wasn't aiming at me, but the person he was after was somewhere around 20 feet from me. The guy with the gun is running after another boy, and the boy being chased runs right past me. I heard about six or seven shots, and I ran around the building, The boy being chased was directly in front of me. After the shots were fired, the boy they were after got away, and I don't know what happened to the guys that were shooting.

Like I said, this situation really messed me up. I remember watching the news a few days later, and more shooting and craziness kept happening. I don't know what happened but I lost it. All I know is one day I woke up and I couldn't talk. Fear had gripped me so hard that I froze. My parents took me to the doctor and they couldn't do anything for me. They gave me medication, and I remember someone at the hospital saying to my mother "Your son will just have to relieve himself from the anxiety and come out of this shock on his own".

It was several days, maybe even a week or two before my speech came back, but I remember shaking in my grandmother's arms, I was a mess. This was serious, I don't remember how many times my parents took me to the doctor, but I do remember that they were distraught; they had no idea what was wrong with me, because I couldn't speak. I literally remember trying to force myself to talk; nothing would come out of my mouth. But by the grace of God I made a full recovery. I know my mother's and my grandmother's prayers are what pulled me through. My family really loved on me, my entire family, from sisters to cousins, everyone really showed me how awesome it is to have others care for you.

It was this love that killed the fear and one day I just snapped out of it.

Getting back to the issue of the process of growing up brings to mind one major question every teenager asks during some point during the puberty process. Who am I? Whether you will admit it or not, if you are out of the teenage years, you probably asked this question. The question that I have found is more appropriate during this time of our lives is, "What will I allow into my life to shape my future?" I knew I was tired of being broke. I knew I was tired of mediocrity. I knew I wanted to live life in a way that I would be excited to wake up in the morning. I will tell you teenagers this: Lifeism # 2 *The faster you mentally determine you are unhappy with your current circumstance, the more time you have to change it*.

You have the power to spend your time wisely, or spend your time foolishly. You have the opportunity, to shape your future today. As a wise man, once told me "Mistakes will be made in life, but always remember the earlier you make them, the more time you have in life to correct them".

Our youth is a precious time, it is fleeting, many in this world, including those in the Hollywood crowd, have spent time talking about ways to stay young, and how so many of us desire the glory of our younger days.

I am wise enough to know that all of this great knowledge and sound judgment may not be received be some, but I am also wise enough to know that in my youth, those that were wiser than me, were the one's I sought out. I don't believe these words I have written are for everybody. At the same time, the young people that heed these words perhaps will be the one's writing books for the generations following us all.

Opportunities are not missed; they are simply passed along to the person paying attention!

Chapter 3: Eliza

Words cannot adequately describe the value and significance of the legacy a grandparent provides. My grandmother Eliza Bridges (pronounced E-ly-za) was an extraordinary woman. Born December 2nd 1909 in Brooksville Mississippi she had over thirty grand and great grandchildren but I knew I was special to her, I knew this because my grandmother loved me individually. This was all that mattered. So to all the grandmothers reading this, remember your love towards your grandchildren matters more than you will ever know. My mother told me the story of how my grandmother reacted when she saw me for the first time. She would tell me this story time and time again.

The story went like this: When my parents brought me home from the hospital, it was a special occasion obviously; the birth of a child is special in and of itself. However, I was the baby, the youngest of three and the only boy, so to my parents, grandparents and family, it was extra special, so I was told.

When my mother went to my grandmother's house, my grandmother –Eliza was doing her normal thing, gardening, and singing.

My mother gave me to my grandmother Eliza, and she said, "My-that is a fine baby". Perhaps this seems insignificant. Not from my perspective, to me this was magical. I know that words have meaning: that is what God says in his word- The Bible. Now if you believe something other than the bible that is OK. too, that is the beauty of it all. We all have the power to choose. So please don't let my beliefs interfere with yours, or interfere with your enjoyment of reading this book.

My grandmother shaped my life with her words that she spoke early on in my life, and it doesn't seem like much, but it has become my destiny. It has become my destiny in that today, I am a successful author, entrepreneur and professor. Parents, you must watch what you speak over your children; there is power in your words.

I remember vividly the inspiration and motivation that my grandmother provided for me at a young age. One memory that stands out was her passion for nature. One day she wanted to go fishing, and I wanted to go with her.

She told my grandfather "Pop", (more about him next chapter), that she wanted to go fishing, and the next day I went with her. My grandmother's idea of fishing may have been a bit different than what you or I may imagine.

Eliza was from Mississippi or the "dirty south" as the young people call it today. When she said she wanted to go fishing that meant if you wanted to tag along you had to "let go of the bed" (granny' phrase) at 4:00am. She wanted to go to Crystal Lake in Mahomet, IL; this was about a 20-minute drive. She also wanted to be at the lake before sunrise in order to start fishing before it got too hot. To her this was the best time, because she believed the fish would bite better, if you started fishing during the cool of the morning. The magical part about it was she was right. I don't know what it was about this time of the morning, but she always caught bunches of bluegills during the wee hours of the morning. I know the time of day was only one part of why she caught all the fish she did. Another reason she was able to catch fish, is she had a special connection to nature and the land.

Another example of how I know this connection she had was one of a kind, was my grandmother's pet squirrel "lady".

You read that correctly, her __"pet" – squirrel! Let me tell you another little story. During one summer I remember staying with my grandmother, and waking up unusually early one day. My grandfather was in the kitchen as usual. As I crawled out of bed, I started looking for my grandmother, and eventually found her outside sitting on the ledge in front of her house. She had this awesome persona. Imagine a 75 year old, caramel-skinned, white-haired, lady rocking back and forth twiddling her thumbs at 6:00 am in the morning.

    She was a beautiful woman. She wore glasses and she always smelled great. If you can't tell I loved my grandmother, as a matter of fact I still do deeply love her, (I know I will see her in heaven years from now). As I walked out the door I heard her humming to herself, she was probably humming some old time church hymn. "Morning Granny, how are you doing this morning", I said. "Fine baby, what are you doing up so early?" she asked. "I don't know I just got up", I explained to her. Although I don't remember much more about what we said to one another I remember what happened next like it was yesterday, and it happened 30 years ago.

My grandmother was an amazing woman, and I knew she had a unique spirit but when she told me she was calling her "squirrel". I thought granny was a little off her rocker. I remember giving her a look like, what are you talking about, and she said. "Look in the tree up there". And wouldn't you know it; I heard a bunch of leaves rustling and out of the huge oak tree in her front yard you could see the small image of a squirrel coming down the tree. I just didn't believe the squirrel was coming to her, maybe it was just running around. No, even with me standing there, an unfamiliar person, as she started calling out "lady" "lady" "lady" the squirrel came from the top of the tree down the branches to the roof of the house. The squirrel checked me out for a minute or two but as granny kept calling "lady" the squirrel jumped down onto her shoulder and on to the ledge on the porch of the house and ate out of granny's hand.

As I write about this story as a nearly 40-year-old man, I see what happened that day in a much different light than I did as a young boy. Our elders had a connection to the world, the earth, and each other that we simply don't have today.

I have read stories and heard people of various backgrounds discuss how the elders within their communities were incredible hunters, farmers, inventors etc. The message that I receive from the reflection of this story about granny is that life is much more than material wealth. We must always remember that there is an energy, a power and an essence within all of us placed there by the one that created us; we were designed to rule and have dominion over this earth.

    I don't know what education level my grandmother had but I know she was a skilled seamstress. I remember all around her house she had custom made porcelain dolls, designer pillows, blankets, and even clothing she had sewed. I still am in awe of how my grandmother illustrated all of the skill she had with little or no training. This ability to do so much with so little illustrates that our youth of today need to understand on a deeper level what they are capable of, what their heritage is. My grandmother was the daughter of a sharecropper. For those who are unfamiliar with sharecropping, after slavery was abolished in the southern United States (1865) landowners would often allow former slaves, the sharecroppers, to use the land to farm and in return they would give a portion of the crop back to the landowner.

As I was saying about granny, she possessed all of this natural ability and she was not college educated, she wasn't trained to do most of what she did, but she developed the skills that she naturally saw within herself and used it to grow and provide for herself. Conversely, many of the youth of today, have all of the technology that they could possibly want, and yet their mindset is that someone owes them something.

Oftentimes, young people don't want to work and they are unwilling to put their natural ability through the rigor of an education to develop their raw talent into something that can provide them an income. Fundamentally, the solution is simply to encourage our young people get an education right? If we can get them in school, then perhaps we can change their mentality. Even though that is possibly the solution, my fear for the younger generation however is that often times, they lack the character and tools such as honor, self-respect, and humility to cultivate a positive self-image. I believe we may have a deeper problem than a lack of education problem.

To all of the young people reading this book who desire to make an impact on their generation, I encourage you to listen to your inner voice. If you feel you are a leader, take a leadership position no matter how large or small within your community and change the minds and hearts of as many within your community as possible. Find someone younger than you and help to mentor and guide him or her to the right path for their life.

What does this have to do with my grandmother? Through her example of taking her raw talent and ability and profiting from it without training, she taught me to become a successful entrepreneur, business professional, academic leader, author and scholar. She also taught me I have the power to create something of value, something that someone else would be willing to pay me for it.

My grandmother was also a woman of prayer, and a virtuous woman who honored family, God, and the importance of teaching the younger one's in the family and community they could accomplish their goals. I remember hearing my grandmother praying all the time. I truly believe that it was the results of her prayers that so many of the trials and difficulties others faced just passed over me.

There is probably someone that has studied this phenomenon from a cultural and spiritual viewpoint, that is the way in which the elders in our community prayed and sought God on behalf of the younger generation.

Growing up I saw so many young people around me falling prey to drugs, gang violence. Seeing so many other forms of negativity all around me, these things existed they were strong influences, but survived it all. I am not a scholar on the topic of cultural history and wonder, is that experience normal? My guess is the answer to that question is no. My mother would tell me she also believed that because granny prayed for us that many things passed over us.

My mom would tell me about times when she would hear granny (as we sometimes called her) praying for the family, sometimes for hours at a time. For this sacrifice I say granny, I love and bless you. I dedicated my doctoral research to my grandmother, and I am actually beginning to tear up as I write this because without the foundation granny provided I wouldn't be who I am today.

If you are a grandparent, please understand your power, your grandchildren, value your time influence and love just as much as you love and adore your grandchildren.

It has also become apparent to me that the day and time that we live in, this 'information and technology age', has choked the life out of our connections. Our community connection, our friendship connections, our spiritual connections and our family connections have all been affected by the era in which we live.

As I write this I understand that I am accountable for the words I write. I try and live as an example as a leader and not a follower and my desire is to do the things about which I write. We must spend the time instilling the wisdom of our past, encouraging the youth of day, and uplifting the young minds to achieve the greatness they have inside of them.

We must never become too enthralled in technology or the speed of the time in which we live in today to teach our young people the lessons we have already learned to ensure the brightness of their future.

Notes

*Fear is **F**alse, **E**vidence, **A**ppearing, **R**eal!*

Chapter 4: "Pop"

Reflecting back on my life as a young man from a small town in Illinois there are so many lessons that I have learned along the way. Many of the lessons I didn't even realize I was learning at the time I was learning them, for whatever reason. Perhaps I was too preoccupied with trivial childish things or just wasn't paying attention altogether. My grandfather was one of the people who taught me many things and I am confident he knew exactly what he was doing. Because he only went through the third grade he wasn't very good at expressing himself.

Let me tell you a little bit about my grandpa, if you haven't picked up on it yet, I called him "Pop". He was born September 5th 1917 in Naxubee County Mississippi the seventh of 12 children. It's about 4:00 a.m. and the house is dead silent, no one is awake, no one except Pop he is getting out of bed and heading straight for the kitchen.

Even though I was one of the people asleep I watched my grandfather go through this routine enough to know that he was up and he was cooking one of his favorite combinations – corn bread, sausage (Hickory Farms) rice, and eggs.

Pop grew up in Brooksville, Mississippi and knew about hard work. He was up that early because for years he used to work at the old Decatur, IL General Motors Steel Plant. He told me how hard this work was the steel was molten hot and they poured it from old fashioned cast iron like buckets. The work was back breaking.

I've heard other people talk about how someone in their family, typically a grandfather, a grandmother, an uncle, generally someone older than they were taught them about hard work. The question is when the uncle, or grandfather taught the lesson did the person being taught learn the lesson, and then apply the knowledge from the lesson to their life? This is one aspect of life that many seem to miss, I believe based on the successes I have had that life's lessons are only effective once the lesson is applied consistently over time to one's life. Lifeism# 3 *Information without application is like a building without a roof- incomplete!* For example, when my grandfather talked to me about his days as a construction worker on the assembly hall arena, where the University of Illinois basketball teams plays, this was truly had work. He talked about long days in the hot sun, and back in the 1950s or 1960s the technology for construction was not as it is today. I took this information and decided that if I wanted to have resources like my grandfather I must determine that I will work hard as well. I will go into more detail regarding hard work versus "working smart" as you may hear people say in a more detailed discussion in Chapter 8.

    I recall my grandfather took me hunting one time. I was only about twelve years old or so, and I was so excited. I remember the night before we were supposed to go, I was so excited, I had never been hunting, and was so curious.

My father is a minister. He is laid back and is not the outdoors type. So for me to experience this side of life, it would only come from Pop. My grandfather had a huge rifle that he kept in the closet in his bedroom. It was right there, so from time to time I would pick it up, and I was so afraid he would see me touch it, I held it literally for 5 seconds and dropped it back in its exact spot like it was a hot potato. But tomorrow I would get to shoot the gun, whooooa!

As we were driving I am asking all kinds of questions like, "what did you shoot at when you were in the Army, Pop? "How many times do you go hunting"? All kinds of questions, I really don't remember all that I asked, but I do remember that the wooded area we were hunting in was a long way away. We left Pop's house at 4:30 a.m. and I was so sleepy. When I am sleepy I get goofy and just talk, so I know my granddad was over me about 20 minutes into the trip.

We finally got to the woods and it was like I was in a movie, I was grinning so big I felt like my face was going to stretch or something. I just couldn't stop smiling. I asked Pop about squirrels and how could kill something that small. That is when I learned that shotguns fire pellets that spray and can hit a target three or four feet across. I was thinking cool; let's blow some stuff up God dogit!!!

After I saw Pop kill two or three squirrels he said, "OK, look right over there" I said "OK. I'm looking… but what I am I looking for?" He said "bub, (don't ask, o.k. that was his nick name for me, I will explain it later) did you see that big muskrat?"

"No, Pop I didn't" I explained. So he pointed my head in the direction of the biggest rat-like thing I have ever seen, I didn't think it was normal muskrat it was big. Maybe it wasn't a muskrat, whatever it was it was huge, a blackish and gray color, and it was sitting perfectly still on an old stump of a really large tree. "Here you go, Bub, now aim right at it and just squeeze the trigger," Pop said. That's exactly what I did, BAAAAM, got it on the first shot! It flew into about nine different pieces, it was absolutely wonderful!. Lesson learned… CONFIDENCE…! If you just do something, you can accomplish what you set your mind to do. Even more, I learned that you don't always have to have all this training and skill, sometimes, you just have to BELIEVE!.

It's been so long ago, so I don't remember the whole conversation we had on the way back to Urbana, Illinois, but I know I was smiling during the whole time. Wow! What a wonderful experience.

This brings me to a thought that is occurring to me just now. If you are a Dad a Uncle, a cousin a man that has younger boys or men in your family, YOU have power to shape their lives. I heard

Dr. Mark Chironna say recently that one of the most detrimental issues affecting the family today is the lack of affirmation from fathers. Daughters and sons just want to know that they matter, and it's great if mom says it, but it is nothing like when daddy says it. So if you are a young woman or a young man and your father never affirmed you, by the prophetic power vested in me from father God and Jesus Christ, <u>You Are Loved, You Are Powerful, You Are Beautiful</u>. Not because I said so, but because your heavenly father does: he just used me to tell you.

    I can recall so many conversations that Pop and I had. He and I hung out all the time. I couldn't tell you what it was, but it was something so significant about spending time with this man. Again, my father is terrific, and I have gleaned much from him as well, but my grandfather's confidence in his manhood spoke to the inner man in me as a young boy. I wanted to be strong like him, I wanted to be a provider like him, and I wanted to be fearless like him. I remember he and I were talking one day and he said "Home comes first".

    Pop was not an educated man. I don't remember who told me, but someone in the family said he only had a third-grade education.

So when Pop talked he was well spoken, but he wasn't giving, long elaborate explanations; it was straight to the point. We were talking about money and providing for the family. Pop was a Deacon, and served in church, but was talking with me about the fact that many Christians give all their money to church and come home to nothing. He taught me not to do this, he said to take care of my home and family and never forget about God and God's work. This is what my grandfather taught me, and I'll leave it at that.

I remember when I was older and I attended an event where a lot of influential people were in attendance, and I was reminded of yet another lesson Pop taught me. As I was speaking to different people at the party I met an older black man, well dressed and seemed to be have it together. A friend of mine introduced us and walked away, and this gentlemen and I started chatting, you know sports, work, and the usual sorts of things men talk about.

I was in my late twenties at the time and this was a man probably in his fifties or older. He asked me my name I told him Charles Bridges III. He looked at me and said, "You're Charlie Bridges grandson" I said, Yes sir, " You come from good stock boy, don't lose what you have, I know you Uncle your dad,

I know most of your people, you have a good family" he explained.

Just at that moment these words that Pop told me rang in my head: "I have a good name in this town boy, I spect you to keep it that way." I was feeling very good about myself, but I knew this was a real learning moment for me. My grandfather had laid the foundation for my success, and all I had to do was keep the good name I already had. There is a biblical reference to this concept found in Ecclesiastes 7:1 "A good name is better than precious ointment, and the day of death better than the day of birth". Lifeism# 4 **Remember having a good reputation is worth more, than having money in the bank.** It seems intuitive, but let me explain this Lifeism further. If your reputation is in tact, and you fall on difficult times, it is that much easier to rise out of that circumstance, with a good reputation than without one. There is so much more to say about the way people perceive you but I will stop here for now.

I recall Pop teaching me about priorities as well. Growing up in the church, in the black church oftentimes, ministers were constantly talking about offering and raising money. My grandfather knew this, and knew that I was being raised in the church. One day he explained to me that my home comes first.

He said if you give the church all your money, then the church has all your money, what sense does that make? For the Christians reading the book, I abide by the tithing mandate and sow financial seeds regularly, so don't take what Pop was saying out of context. He was not referring to your financial obligations to your community church. What he was teaching is that people who are out of balance when it relates to giving will be out of balance in their personal finances. Perhaps you didn't grow up in church, but regardless this principle is relevant.

Many of us have heard about money principles all of our lives. One thing I have noticed is that success principles don't change, but we must. Sounds like a Lifeism. Yes it is Lifeism # 5 ***Success principles don't change, but we must.*** How many times have we heard you must have financial priorities and you need to save for retirement? The way I see this is, it is the universe's way of getting information inside our core. Have you ever seen a movie a few times, and then on the last time you watched, you notice, "hey I never saw that before?" Such is life, and its principles for success. We are bombarded with the ideals and guiding elements of success until either we give in or not. It is up to us.

I wonder how many of my brothers reading this, were missing positive male role models when they were growing up. I know that in my life, I have had countless conversations that have shown me that those that have lost time with fathers have deep pain. As I have listened to several counseling professionals on this topic, it seems obvious to me there is no escaping the need for that fatherly love. I know I just addressed the issue of a father's affirmation, but another aspect of having daddy around is not the affirmation at all, it is his presence. I know some of you have felt or still feel rejected, feel your self-esteem has suffered as a result of your father's not being in your lives. I don't know what that pain is like because I was blessed to have my dad in my life.

Although, I can't speak about the pain, I can speak on your future. We all have choices. We can choose to be a victim or victor, bitter or better, a champion or a failure. I challenge anyone male or female who experienced the pain of not having daddy. I challenge you with the mission to help those that cross your path to overcome this adversity.

If you have experienced the pain of growing up without your father, or with limited attention from him, you are in a position to help others overcome this pain, if you choose to help them. You can help those with the same pain you have felt and find peace within yourself, filling that void with God's love for you and becoming a success. You can become a success in whatever way you determine, and afterwards find someone who was struggling as you were.

You can show them the path you took to overcome your individual situation. Lifeism #6 ***Once you are able to, give back, in anyway you can, no matter how large or how small.*** I firmly believe many of the challenges we face in our lives are for two main purposes. I believe that there could be other purposes, but the two that I am refereeing to here, I believe are the primary reasons for our struggles. The first reason is to develop our character and strength. Perhaps you can think of a very devastating situation you faced, and while you were in that dilemma the world seemed to crumble. However, on the other side of the issue, you felt something on the inside of you change, right? Somehow, you just knew that you changed, that you have stepped into a new dimension of your own strength and knowledge of who you were.

Oftentimes, we are tested, and during these tests we see what we can endure. Although we may try and avoid the pain, the pain is what causes the strength to develop. Just as an athlete who hates to lift weights, doesn't enjoy the pain from the pressure of the weight, we don't like the pressure of life. But as the saying goes "no pain….no gain".

The other reason I believe we go through things that seem so hurtful or unfair is that the pain we feel will help someone else. I believe that sometimes God decides things will work out in a way that causes us pain so that the seemingly negative situations we deal with will better equip those in our lives navigate through their individual processes. I will talk about the process that we often have to go through later, but dealing with something that someone else has gone through sometimes makes it just a little easier.

Find someone who has what you want, do you what they do, and you'll get what they have.

Chapter 5: Which way to turn? (Choices)

As I said earlier this entire book is dedicated to the idea that success can be yours by finding out what **_not_** to do. Obviously, there is no "silver bullet" and there is not just one thing required for you to reach your full potential. However, there is the fact that I have been successful, successful defined by my standards, not society's standards. My accomplishments came from the foundation of understanding that it is not about having a wealthy family, or having great connections, but a strong work ethic, sound judgment, good relationships and an understanding that I can learn from other's mistakes.

In High School the real understanding of this principle of avoiding the mistakes others made began to take shape. What I found was that things began to get very real in my life. I found that reality was beginning to sink in, I was a teenager, but I understood that I wouldn't be a teenager forever. Eventually I would go from teenager, to a 20-year old, and then a 30-year old and so on.

By that meant I would have to be doing something worthwhile, including working on planning a life. Here is when the notion of developing a vision for my life began to take shape. I started to think about that fact that if I wanted to achieve something other than living in poverty and having a low income level, it was up to me. This is true for you as well. It sounds like a no brainer, but, it's not as simple a principle as it sounds. There are many people who feel that they will be given support by this source or another, but in this life "if it's to be it's up to me." So… get up, get out there and get it done. Don't ask for what you want, decide what you want, and find out what is required to have it and go get it!

Speaking of High School I recall an experience I had when I was playing basketball during my freshman and sophomore years. I was a short guy in high school but I had some "hops" and "handles" on the basketball court. More importantly I learned to lean on my inner voice to make the right choices. I was jealous of many of the favorite ball players on the team. The favorites I refer to are the boys that the coaches loved and seemed to cater to. I began to understand how "politics" could affect the opportunities people are given in life.

I saw that boys who played were taller and more skilled, and it played and it was hard to argue with. I also saw that some boys were talented but needed to be coached to achieve a higher skill level. They rarely got a chance to improve, either in practice or on game night. More importantly than what happened on the basketball court was what happened off the basketball court. I learned this first hand one day after practice. On this day one of the starters and I were messing around in the locker room. We were talking girls, movies, what can I say, jock talk. He went into his locker and pulled out a vial with white powder in it. I don't remember the entire conversation, I just remember thinking OMG, this is crazy.

To make a long story short I saw how bad choices can cost you. Sometimes, they could cost you your life. The young man who showed this to me, may read this book, and so let me just say this. I know that the fact that he was involved with drugs impacted his life, and the opportunities he was afforded. One of the other star players was involved with drugs and it cost him opportunity to play college basketball. These two young men had serious potential, I can honestly say, if they could have had the proper coaching, they could have excelled in college and perhaps beyond.

This is not a new conversation. We need our kids to stay off drugs, and to wait to have sex. The question is, do they do what they should?. My two boys are going to have to make the same decisions I did when I was growing up. What are the factors that determine successful outcomes when our young people begin to have to make choices? I know for a fact many times, young people from good families, go the wrong way. I know that young people who are taught the *right* way still go the *wrong* way.

I believe that the individual child must make an individual decision to be whatever it is they want to be. Deep down, I believe most people are choosing what direction they are taking. Perhaps someone who is a professional psychologist can explain this phenomenon.

Although I am not a trained psychologist, I understand people, I have been successful, and have watched people's lives, and that is why I wrote this book. I am convinced- one of the most important keys for success is the power of the choice. Somehow, when we mentor, or teach young people we have to stress the importance of the fact that we cannot live for them, that at the end of the day, it is up to them to decide.

Lifeism #7 **Every person's destiny is in their own hands. We all have the capacity to shape our own futures with the choices of today.**

Speaking of choices let me address one issue that has plagued many in the African American community for years. Self-identity. There are countless numbers of African American scholars, scientists, inventors and individuals who have been applauded for their accomplishments. Yet many in the black community think that blacks are supposed to be less intelligent for some reason. Growing up I had to deal with the choice of fitting in with the crowd or deciding to be my own man.

Going with the crowd would have possibly given me a better social life, but I discovered my identity early on. I credit my mother mainly with speaking into my spirit and mind that I was intelligent and I was valuable. She always told me how smart I was. She would say things like, "You make me so proud to be your mother. I love how you think, how you treat me as your mother, you are just a fine young man".

I don't believe my mother's affirmation was the only thing that shaped my ability to identify who I was early on.

For whatever reason, I believe it was just God's grace. I learned how to spend time alone and reflect at an early age. During these times, I decided that I would accomplish greatness. I just chose it!! So in high school when others were partying and goofing off in school, I did my work and made the honor roll every year. I graduated with a GPA that surpassed the GPA system of the school an A+ average. I chose to allow my intelligence to shine.

This is my message to young people or anyone who feels that they don't have what it takes to succeed because it will require the tough choices. If you allow someone else's affirmation or definition of who you are to shape your thinking, you have given that person control over your future. It's O.K. to be successful, even if grandma and auntie don't understand it or even condemn it. It's OK. to want more than what you have now. You don't have to have someone else's approval to achieve something. You only need your work ethic, determination, and a plan!

Proverbs 6: 8 says: *"Go to the ant, O sluggard; consider her ways, and be wise. Without having any chief, officer, or ruler, she prepares her bread in summer and gathers her food in harvest"*. This scripture is two sentences but is so rich in its content. It is about, work ethic, choices, self discipline, prioritization, proper planning, laziness, wisdom among other things all in one verse. I must digress for a moment; I am often in awe of the Bible. So many scripture verses are compact with so much wisdom and knowledge. It truly is a marvel.

O.k., back to my point, choices, our environment so often determines choices. The company we keep often impacts our choices, the music we listen to, the positive or negative we allow in all have direct affects on the directions we choose. Have you ever awakened said a good prayer, if you pray, had a good conversation with your spouse, and the rest of the day went so fast that it seemed unreal? In fact, during the day things just flowed, you were happy, you got things done, and you just felt on your game. Conversely, you've likely had that day where you woke up in a bad mood, your energy was just not there, and you didn't fight it off. Someone gave you bad news at work, and people complained around you all day. We can't help having bad days, we don't control what happens around us, but we control our attitude about what happens around us. Sounds like another Lifesim #8, ***Attitude determines our perspective, and our level of elevation or deterioration.***

I am certain there is a scientific explanation and a scholarly literary base on the topic of decision making. This book is not about that, this is a practical simplistic discussion of what choices we are to make and how we decide to make those choices. Recently I had conversation with a young man who has a family but was torn between deciding to continue to work a job that could take his attention from school or focus his efforts on school. As I discussed his options, I recalled all the times I had an opportunity to decide to pursue a life without my education.

I believe those choices would have been mistakes, because my education has opened several doors, that would have been closed otherwise. Please do not misunderstand me, there are many people who don't succeed with education as their primary focus. Although many of them made it prior to the year 2000, the fact remains that if you are not highly educated there still is a place for you to be a productive member of society.

However, you still need skills, no matter your education level, but that is a discussion for another chapter. The conversation this young man and I had, centered on his decision, which was a big one, but he was having this discussion with someone who believes in education.

Therefore, my approach in addressing his decision was the long-term benefits of education versus the rewards of income provided by the job he then had. The choice remained his decision; however the influence he allowed into his sphere of influence impacted his decision.

Perhaps someone reading this does not have positive influences in their life. Maybe you have a situation where there is negativity all around you. It could be your family doesn't support you, and you feel as though you've never had support in your decision-making. You may be asking how do I make choices with positive influence if there is nothing but negativity surrounding me? I cannot relate entirely because my youth was not filled with complete negativity; there were elements of positivity. However, there was enough negativity around me to speak to this dilemma.

I had to choose, to do things that would propel me forward. If that meant just reading a book about something in life that I wanted, I did just that. When I would read magazines about wealthy people, or just watching television that put the lifestyle I wanted in from of me, I absorbed the images into my spirit and soul. Let's be clear- this conversation is not solely about material gain.

I knew that I wanted more, and that included the resources I needed to live a fulfilling, healthy and happy life. If you are dealing with a depressing environment, watch comedy. If there is violence in your neighborhood, spend time in a park or at a relative's home where there is a least some peace. I firmly believe that if we choose to move in a positive direction, the universe supports our positive desires.

As an educated man, I would love to have a more in depth discussion of decision making. I would enjoy talking about the various types of decisions we make, choosing our spouses, our career paths, our hobbies, and even those we call our friends.

However, when I think about those I believe are reading this book, I feel that people want to develop the right habits and the right attitude first. If that is not the case, it is my view that this is what you should want to develop first. Have you heard the saying "Watch your thoughts; they become words. Watch your words; they become actions. Watch your actions; they become your habits. Watch your habits; they become character. Watch your character; it becomes your destiny"?

It is my understanding there is confusion as to who originally said this, so for the sake of this discussion we won't concern ourselves with the author, but rather the content. No matter the author, these words ring true in my view. Even if you are in a position in life that is not the position you desire, choose to keep your mind focused on who and what you want to become, and choose to work towards BECOMING just that!!

Often when we see success in others, we are not jealous of their success, but frustrated that we have not achieved the same results.

Chapter 6: Mr. Anderson- My Mentor

Imagine you are a young black man in a college town in the Midwest, with no money, no "connections," no "well-off" family members, and living in poverty. Now imagine that you have a dream, you have a dream of "making it" outside of this community you're in, a dream of making a good living, perhaps making a name for yourself one day, doing something that people will pay attention to. Continue in this same line of thinking and now you come to a point in your thoughts where reality sets in, how do you actually get out of being broke? How do you get into college? How do you "make it"? Well, I didn't have all of the answers on paper; I just knew that *somehow* I would be OK. Don't ask me how, I just knew, I believe it was that inner voice that I've talked about all along that was always giving me a peace about my life.

As often as the difficulties of finding the how to a problem are in our lives, as many of you well know, just as often the how just works itself out. Well, one of the ways that I believe God helped me to be OK. was allowing me to meet one man.

This man was already successful, already enjoyed a good lifestyle, and took time out of his life to help someone else. Lifeism #9 ***Once you are able to, give back, in anyway you can, no matter how large or how small.*** This Lifeism has a particular significance because it meant the difference between me learning many lessons, I wouldn't have learned otherwise.

Mr. Anderson, no, not the one from *The Matrix*, became one of the most instrumental pieces to my success puzzle. He was my mentor, but he didn't tell me he wanted to mentor me, I decided that if I was going to learn to be successful, I needed to learn from people who were already successful. Here is another Lifeism #10 ***"find someone in life who has what you want, do what they do, and you will get what they have"***. Mr. Anderson was a well-respected businessman in my town, that found success and shared much of what he knew with me, and I am forever grateful for his love and support. As I am writing about Mr. Anderson, I have remembered something I want to share with you. I will continue telling you about Mr. Anderson in a moment.

After all the lessons Mr. Anderson had taught me and all the encouragement he showed me, I remember one lesson that hit me like a ton of bricks. Mr. Anderson didn't teach me about humility, he didn't tell me how to appreciate taking life in steps but Mr. Miller did. After I graduated from college, I wanted to get to work, and there were not very many corporate opportunities in my town. So I decided to interview for an assistant manager position at McDonald's. I didn't want to work at McDonald's after college, I thought I should be doing something more, but I went to the interview to see what I may find. I was interviewing with Mr. Miller, a black man who owned probably four or five McDonald restaurants in the town, I would guess he was doing very well for himself.

During the interview Mr. Miller began to ask me why I wanted to work at McDonald's. I told him I thought the company was a great organization and that I knew they had a strong track record of success. I also said that I honestly didn't think I would be working at McDonald's after college but I wanted to learn more about the company before closing a door.

Mr. Miller didn't take kindly to my remark. He asked if I have ever been an assistant manager; at that point, I had not. The next thing he said to me, truly changed my whole perspective, I would have to say it is another Lifesim #11 ***"The moment you begin to understand that the world doesn't revolve around you, your perspective is prepared for success"***.

Mr. Miller told me, "Charles you are a bright young man, but you expect things to go your way, just because you want them to, and that is not the way things work". I sat back in my chair with the wind knocked out of my sails. Mr. Miller actually ended the interview prematurely because I think he felt I was arrogant. Guess what? He was right: I was arrogant. I was arrogant, and I felt the world owed me something.

The world doesn't owe me anything, and the world doesn't owe you anything. God gave you life and he expects something in return. Wow, another Lifeism #12 ***"Life is God's gift to you, what you do with your life, is your gift to God"***. Please understand, many of the Lifeisms or life principles I am sharing with you, are things that I may have read or heard from someone.

I wish I was that smart, but the truth is I am smart enough to know that there are many people smarter than me.

OK that was a long story to tell prior to talking about the man this chapter is all about-Mr. Anderson. Mr. Anderson was the father of one of my teammates on my high school basketball team. His son and I were pretty cool, and as I recall it, after one of the games his son introduced me. Little did I know that this connection would be of great significance to my personal and professional development. As I was telling you earlier the fact that I was a young black man in a community that was at times openly discriminatory against blacks, made me feel trapped. Meeting Mr. Anderson was not that special to me at first. In my mind he was just another white man, I didn't know if he was prejudiced against blacks, but I always had my guard up.

One evening after our game during my sophomore year, Mr. Anderson and I bumped into each other after I came out of the locker room. I will never forget this conversation. We were standing near the concession counter just chatting, and he said "You know Charles, if you need help when the time comes to get into college I want you to know I would be happy to help you".

I know we talked about much more than that, but that one sentence was a tremendous motivation and vote of confidence. I thought to myself, wow; I must have some sort of blessing from the heavenly father to have a white man trying to help this young black kid. I know many people don't think in terms of race or color, but that was my honest thought back then.

So our relationship began. What was interesting is that from what I remember getting into college was something I accomplished almost completely on my own. Mr. Anderson really started supporting me once I was in school. I don't know if he did that on purpose, but no matter how it happened, I was accepted, into the University of Illinois at Urbana Champaign. From time to time Mr. Anderson would come by my parents' home and take me to lunch, sometimes three or four times a month. I remember during my junior and senior years in college we talked all the time. Every time I would achieve a level of success, we would celebrate; he would wine and dine me (so to speak), encourage me, and teach me what he knew about success. After a while I got really nervous I thought this is too good to be true, this white man wants something from me.

So one day at lunch I decided that enough is enough and I needed to get the questions I had off my chest. I needed to know what was going on with Mr. Anderson and why he was being so nice to me. So, as we were eating, I just asked him, straight to the point, "Mr. Anderson, as much as I appreciate you and all your help and support, why? Why are you mentoring me and helping me so much?" He smiled; He had this smile that I thought lit up a room. He had a charm about him that was undeniable, and as I was asking him the question the look on his face was as if he was expecting this question, and he was thinking, "So you finally got the nerve to ask me."

Perhaps I will never know what he was thinking, but that is how he looked at me. He said, and I will put this in quotations but this is not his exact words (in fact many of the quotes are not exactly as people said them, I write as I recall). "Charles, I remember watching your basketball games, and when you came out onto the court, you stood out. Every time you were on the court, you were hustling. You were always scrambling for the ball and trying to make things happen, and I like that.

In fact that is what I believe it takes to make it in this world. You have to hustle, not only that, white people have all the resources in this country; white people are the dominant group in this nation. So, its my belief that if others are to become more successful than those in power, white Americans must help those who don't always have the tools for success:" I was amazed at his words, I remember feeling like crying, but I didn't.

From there, our relationship continued to flourish. Now I had a better understanding of where he was coming from. I saw this man was not in it for himself, and that made sense because he was already successful. Now I trusted him, and I believed his intentions were honest. Lifeisms #13 ***"If your intent is to truly do good, your life outcome will in turn produce good".*** I took that Lifeism from the Bible, as God said that we all reap what we sow. I think it is important you investigate why people are connected to you. I once heard someone say there are four types of people: adders, subtractors, multipliers and dividers. I only have room for adders and multipliers, I only want people around me who are benefiting me, and who are gaining from my involvement in their lives as well.

I am grateful that I was blessed to have someone like Mr. Anderson push me along during a season of my journey when those nudges were truly significant.

There are many types of people reading this book; some of you were fortunate enough to have mentors or people who supported you in your families, while others of you had nothing of the sort. Either way, I want you to take from my experience the fact that Mr. Anderson saw something in me that he thought was a positive trait and he decided to help me because of that. I often tell people when I am coaching or teaching about developing teams or groups in the work place, that it is much simpler to make someone who is a 7 a 10 than it is to make someone who is a 3 a 10. In other words, you have to bring something to the table. In any job or career, your résumé or set of skills is really all you bring to the job.

While Mr. Anderson is the only person who can explain exactly why he chose to help me, I am the only one that truly can describe *how* it helped me. Having someone who was already successful in life, spend his time, his resources, and provide his knowledge to me gave me a heightened level of confidence.

Imagine a young black kid who has a lower income lifestyle, no family members who have attended college, and no environment to foster success. Now imagine someone like Mr. Anderson, a successful Caucasian entrepreneur entering this young man's life and spending his time, and freely giving his knowledge, and exerting his energy to help this individual. Perhaps you can understand why this was so powerful.

You are the most valuable asset you have, and as the laws of attraction that have become so popular explain, you attract what you are. If you desire to attract wealth begin to think wealthy thoughts and surround yourself with images and environments that put you in a prosperous mindset. Prior to Mr. Anderson coming into my life I was only a teenager so I didn't know about vision boards or self talk (If you don't know what these are ask me at a book signing). All I knew was that I wanted to be and do more than what I saw possible within my environment.

As I came of age, I wanted to become someone who created and added to the world around me, and I began to create good habits in an effort to accomplish this on my own.

Somehow as time went on Mr. Anderson found me and began to support me, and it was simply magical. It was magical for me, magical is great, but I also believe you can create this sort of energy in your life for real. If you decide you want to be healthy but right now you are living an unhealthy life style. I am convinced as you began changing what thoughts you put into your mind, and what you believe about yourself, your health will improve as a result of the changes that occur. All the changes that will occur will have resulted from the inner change you started. Everything else is a chain reaction and you have to let the universe take care of that. I guess that saying is really true, "if it is to be it is up to me"!

No matter when tomorrow is, tomorrow holds within it the ability to wipe away all the mistakes of yesterday.

Chapter 7: Is Church Every Day?

After reading six chapters of this book, I am certain you see that my spirituality plays an important role in the way I live life. However, growing up in the church was well, let me just say, it had its drawbacks! To refer to my time growing in church in extremely negative terms is unfair, because my faith has carried me through many difficulties in life. At the same time, dealing with the religious rules and minutiae that churches are often filled with was a pain. Not to mention that as a young person, all I wanted to do was run and play, and laugh and all of the things that children do. So going to church on a Sunday sometimes to three different services, sucked!

For privacy purposes I will not disclose the names of my first church. Some of you know me and know the pastor I grew up learning from and the name of the church. Growing up as a preacher's kid, or PK, as we are often called meant that I was always in church. One nice thing about my church was that my pastor knew a lot of well-known personalities in the gospel community.

People like Shirley Caesar, Marvin Winans, BeBe and CeeCee Winans, Bishop Alfred Owens, and other well-known people visited the church. When these people visited it was opportunity for me as a young person to see what happens outside my little town. This was because oftentimes these ministers and singers would discuss things that happened when they traveled around the United States or the world.

On the other hand, no matter what V.I.P was at my church we were there all the time. Here's a typical weekly service schedule: Sunday School 9:00 a.m., Morning Worship 11:00am, Sunday Night Service 5:00 p.m. (sometimes with a travel destination), Tuesday Night Bible Study, 7:00 p.m., Wednesday Choir Rehearsal 6:30 p.m. Thursday Youth Group Meeting 7:00 p.m., Saturday Fundraisers, Chicken Fry or something, (all day). I am not joking about this schedule. Sometimes there were revivals that were weeklong events and we would rarely take a week off after a revival.

So why did we go to church so much? Honestly, you would need to speak to my parents to find out why they took us so much. In my view now as a black man who has learned a thing or two about the History of African American history in the United States, one reason blacks attended church so frequently is that after slavery they didn't know much else about the world other than that God was someone they needed to look to for help. For the African American community, an often marginalized and oppressed group, dependence on a God for the basic ability to cope with the traumas in the world commonplace. With all that intellectual and intelligent rhetoric regarding the reasons those of African descent church said, it still does not take away from the fact that so much church shapes a person and the way they approach life.

Because I heard about God, and about the way a person should think about God from a Christian perspective at home and then at church and was taught this was the "right" religion this impacted my belief system. I would argue that a person who grows up Methodist, has a high percentage chance of becoming Methodist. A person who grows up Muslim probably would likely be a Muslim and so forth.

What I discovered once I became an adult and in college was that there comes a point when every man or woman, must decide what he or she was taught about religion is true for him or herself.

What I did one semester was I went to the library and got on my computer and started to do some research on various religions. About a week into the research, my inner voice so strongly disapproved of this search, so I stopped. I felt in my heart that I knew what I believed not because my parents told me what I should believe, but because I had worked out my own salvation step by step. I do however; recommend that if you are the type of person that desires the truth, you should take the time to meditate and to compare what you believe to others' thoughts and beliefs. If what you believe feels right in your heart of hearts this will not present any issues.

Conversely if you have doubts about what you believe this time of reflection will bring these doubts to the surface. The young people in my church were a great group of people. In any group of people you have the sour apples, as was the case with the youth in my church. Despite the negative people and the haters, what I discovered by constantly socializing is that you can find out who really has your back, and you can uncover who means you well and who does not. In case you didn't know, people in church oftentimes can be the most critical, hypocritical, insincere, and disloyal people you will find. For whatever reason you can find more evil in God's house than you can outside of it. Now, I understand when people are dysfunctional and have issues, but there is no better place than the house of God. Even with that understanding growing up in church I learned to keep people at a distance until they earn my trust.

What I don't want is the negative people or negative situations that people in the church created to become the centerpiece of the discussion of church. Growing up in church was a memorable experience. My father once said "anytime you deal with people or with the public there will be some sort of drama", I have found this was definitely true.

However, beyond the drama, beyond the schemes and downright treacherous behavior of the so-called "saints of God," was a young man's childhood shaped by spirituality.

For many of us who live in America, we may understand that from a historical perspective religion and the divisions religious groups have caused have been devastating to many societies. However, I would like to focus on what the church means for communities and what church should provide for our families and lives for that matter.

Growing up in church meant I was off the streets and not participating in activities that would have negative outcomes. Often on Friday nights there was some form of church service. While many people were doing there "thing" in the community, engaging in activities that often were unfruitful, I was in church. Don't be confused about this, as a young man; I resented having to be in church all the time, what seemed like everyday. At the same time, church provided me a foundation of beliefs that created a certain perspective throughout my life. This question comes to mind- if young people don't have values, belief systems, nor any sense of responsibility, what does that mean for their lives?

I imagine there are some reading this book who have seen Eddie Murphy's film, *Trading Places*.

If you have not seen the film, the premise of the movie is that a wealthy businessman and a homeless man cross paths and the wealthy businessman's bosses get involved in both the homeless mans' and the businessman's lives. The bosses decide to wager that the homeless man could take the place of the businessman in their firm if given the opportunity. Conversely the wager also predicted the businessman would turn to crime and violence if he lost his job and faced public humiliation. The outcome was that the boss who bet both men would change roles if their environments were changed was right. In the movie the homeless man became an up standing businessman and the businessman took to crime, as a result of various factors the two bosses manipulated.

My point in discussing this film is that my upbringing in the church set the tone for the course of my life. Just as the bosses changed the path of the characters in the Eddie Murphy film through manipulating their environment, my physical environment shaped many of the early elements of my character. As you may know there are many people who are raised well, but then go down dark and disparaging paths in their lives.

However, my perspective remains that no matter one's circumstance, if there is any opportunity for the environment to shift towards positive influence, there is an opportunity to move in a positive direction.

During my years in the church I witnessed, extra marital affairs, rumors of men dying of HIV, leaders manipulating church congregation and those under their authority, conspiracy shaming the reputation of individuals, homosexuality and even drugs and criminal activity all happening in the church. (Homosexuality is a sin in the Christian faith; I know some may practice that lifestyle, however I am simply stating the facts). I saw with my own eyes how people that should be living a life that is pleasing to God, were out for themselves and would do whatever is necessary to get what they wanted.

Once again, throughout all of this negativity, I heard within my soul that this was not a reflection of the God I believed in nor would this chaos have to determine my path in life. I wish I could provide you with a way to tap into this voice within yourself, I am not sure I can do that. What I can do is tell you unequivocally that the voice is there.

This is not a schizophrenic, alter ego that you have, this is your soul, what I believe is God's way of communicating with all of us. As I have said throughout my writings those who don't believe in God do not have to dismiss themselves from this conversation. Even if you don't believe God put this voice there, the voice exists nonetheless. We all know about that "gut feeling" or that the instinctual reaction can be so often the right reaction. Just because I believe it's God and you don't doesn't mean you can't benefit from this perspective.

While growing up in the church I learned about God's system of integrity. Webster defines integrity as "a firm adherence to a code of especially moral or artistic values". You and I may define integrity differently, but I have learned that if you have faith in God, and God has chosen you, there are limits to your ability to stray from the right path. I have heard some call it the "scales of balance" meaning, God's way of making you pay for your choices, the whole notion of "you reap what you sow". However, for the sake of this conversation, let's just called it good old fashion integrity.

There was no mistaking that I understood that stealing was wrong, with the amount of preaching and teaching I heard on the topic. That was one lesson I should have learned, right? I recall somewhere in my teenage years during my time of rebelling against the system that my sister and I decided to take some clothes from a retail clothing store where she worked at. We did quite a bit of damage at this store, no telling exactly how much monetary value was associated with the amount of clothes we stole, but I am confident it was substantial (I can see my sister jaw drop from me telling her business).

To make a very long story short, I recall one day hearing my inner voice tell me that I would have to pay for my actions, because it was required of me to be a man of integrity. It was some time after the entire clothing escapade my sister and I went on, but eventually the first car I bought brand new was repossessed. I was crushed to say the least. When I lost the car, I remember that voice reminding me that I had to pay for my actions. I believe God was letting me know that he was not going to allow me to just do things my own way.

So what is the lesson for us here? Again, this is about my life, but I believe I was given this story, and these experiences to shed light on what may have happened, or is happening to those of you reading this book. The message is simple. There is a system of balance in this universe. I will not call it cause and effect, but I will say that the universe will keep score of your wrongdoings, and at some point you must be accountable for them.

Notes

One four-letter word is always appropriate: WORK!

Chapter 8: Working Hard Versus Working Smart

Remember when I said there is an inner voice that speaks to us, and that one of the main purposes of this book is to help you to focus on that voice and heed its teachings? One of the first things regarding working hard versus working smart came to me while meditating and 'listening' to this voice.

As I was driving, I began to reflect on my professional career. I have worked as an entrepreneur, in various roles in corporate America, and have done so all over the United States. With that experience I have seen how diversity, background, ethnicity, politics, and many other factors impact how people progress in their jobs, and business. The information regarding how certain individuals attain certain achievements may not be as readily available as one may desire. To take it a step further, it has been my experience that the actual process people go through to achieve success is often overlooked. There are seminars that you can pay hundreds, perhaps even thousands of dollars to attend that talk about strategies, techniques and formulas for success.

Regardless, the day to day work that must be completed is something that each of us must *decide* to do on our own. The point I am making is: after the seminar, after the college degree, after the pep talk from whomever, manager, mother or any family member, there is one ingredient that remains that is required to carry us from where we are to where we want to be.

That ingredient is <u>Hard Work</u>. Think about it this way, no matter what career field, industry, or occupation you maintain eventually there is significance work to be done to move upward. Let's say you have not reached the level of success that you want and you are thinking of ways to get there. Let's say you are able to take two weeks off from work and brainstorm about this next level of success you aspire to reach. After the two weeks of time off, and the brainstorming, you have the perfect plan. You have even taken this plan to a friend who has achieved a higher level of success than you have up to this point in your life, and this friend approves of your plan. Now, you take that plan, file it in your desk, and leave it there. What happens? Nothing.

As simple as this principle may seem, there are hundreds, thousands, maybe even millions of people who are dreaming, and hoping of a brighter tomorrow. Their efforts are not matching their level of dreaming. It was Thoreau who said, "Success usually comes to those who are too busy to be looking for it."

How many times, have you heard someone say, don't work hard work smart? If I had a dollar for every person that made that remark to me, I would have more wealth than I have today. So let's talk about the notion of working smart. I am sure there is probably some empirical, or research-based information on what scholars think this concept means, but let's just use our common sense. In my mind, the idea of working smart means that instead of working hard, I am going to find a way to get where things done, and accomplish certain things, with less effort. This sounds a lot like the term "efficiency". Webster defines efficiency as *effective operation as measured by a comparison of production with cost (as in energy, time, and money) or the ratio of the useful energy delivered by a dynamic system to the energy supplied to it.*

What one person takes away from that definition may be different from what another individual gets from the definition. Essentially, what I see in this definition is having a system that allows for production with minimal effort.

Let's look at side-by-side comparison of two hypothetical professionals and how they work differently as it relates to efficiency. Person A is a general contractor, this is someone who owns a business, and builds buildings for profit. This is a very crude and simplified definition, but true nonetheless. If person A doesn't go to work to build buildings there is no profit. If there is no profit there is not success, so the question is how efficient is this profession.

Remember, this all centers around the comparison of working smart versus working hard. Person B, is an insurance agent. An insurance agent like other certain specific types of professions has something built into the way he or she is paid, called residual income. Daily each professional has to execute some level of performance or work to receive pay, correct? If the insurance agent doesn't go and sell insurance products her business doesn't grow, and if the general contractor doesn't build buildings his business is not profitable.

How they get paid once the work is completed is where things get interesting however. Once a building is completed the general contractor, receives a fee. A fee is a percentage that the contractor adds to the bid on the project on which he is working. Once that contractor is paid the fee, there is no additional income from that building.

Conversely, the residual income or passive income that the insurance agent may receive from policies within her book of business can continue to pay her month after month. The insurance agent is paid consistently because the insurance company pays the agent a small percentage usually monthly for all policies in the agent's portfolio. For example hypothetically, and insurance agent with a policy base of 6,000 policies will receive a month income of say $5,500 for no actual performance of effort, but residual pay for work already performed. Would you agree that the insurance agent's situation is more conducive to an income stream with less overall effort? Seems logical right?

The key that I see here is that in either case, the builder has to build the buildings, and the insurance agent has to go and get the policies. Hard work is taking place no matter what, but after the work is performed, what you build can determine how you are compensated. Lifeism #15 ***Never try and escape the required effort necessary to build an income generating system.*** And Lifeism #16 ***Consistently seek ways to have multiple streams of income and passive or residual income.***

If you are like me, and you have read books that discuss ideas about success and ways to prosper, and find that often the ideas are not practical, I have some practical information. Regardless of the profession you choose, regardless of your level of expertise, you must posses a committed stated of mind. Your commitment must be the driving force that sees you through the adversity, and all the roadblocks that tell you, that you will not succeed. Author and Scottish mountaineer W.H Murray said, *"Until one is committed there is hesitancy. The chance to draw back… always in effectiveness. Concerning all acts of initiative (and creation). There is one elementary truth, the ignorance of which kills countless ideas and splendid plans:*

That the moment one definitely commits oneself, then providence moves too. All sort of things occur to help one that would otherwise have never occurred. A whole stream of events issues from the decision, raising in one's favor all manner of unforeseen incidents and meetings and material assistance, which no man could have dreamed would have come his way. I have learned a deep respect for one of the Goethe's couplets: Whatever you can do or dream you can, begin it. Boldness has genius, power and magic in it. Begin it now!"

While fully persuaded regarding the effectiveness of hard work and commitment, I would be remiss were I not to leave room to discuss serendipity. Merriam Webster defines serendipity as the *faculty or phenomenon of finding valuable or agreeable things not sought for.* Yet others say that serendipity is where good fortune and wisdom cross paths. According to a blog within the oxford dictionary, the writer and politician Horace Walpole coined the term in 1754. Mr. Walpole used the term to describe the good fortune the Princes of Serendip experienced throughout their travels in the book *"The Three Princes of Serendip"* authored by Michele Tramezzino in 1557. Essentially as the princes travel through the island on which they were born, their travels were continuously blessed with good fortune. The story ends with all the kings becoming wise rulers.

Serendipity could also be called good fortune, chance, or luck, but no matter what you call it, there is simply no way we can control the way the universe controls things. I don't believe it is simply the universe, I believe in a higher power, a deity, some don't but either way many things are out of our control. Working hard, playing by the rules of the game, may not pay off in the timeframe you or I expect, but in my life I have seen the dividends of hard work, despite the span of time it took for the dividends to come about. I don't believe hard work will pay off for me and not others. Rationally it makes sense that if one person applies a principle and another person applies that same principle there should be similar results.

With that, there is something to be said for the times in life when good things just happen.

Some people believe that these times are random occurrences that simply happen from time to time. I think about it in a different way. My view is that as we consistently orchestrate our lives in a manner that plans for future success, the times of good fortune can be determined not accidentally encountered. Many of us have heard the phrase "If it is to be, it is up to me" well, I believe that phrase applies to the times good things happen.

Think of the scenario of a college student who desires to earn a degree to begin a career. The student studies hard, sacrifices time with friends, and spends late nights preparing for exams. No one else is doing the work for the college student. If the student is to graduate she must put in the work, right? Yes, that is right, and to take it further, once the student has studied and learned the material being taught, has passed the exams and graduates, the student must look for career opportunities. It would be wonderful if companies were just knocking on the student's door, but generally speaking this is not how it works. If the student wants all the hard work she put into earning that education to pay off with a career, she must find that career opportunity and prove to those hiring her she is the best out of all those applying for the position.

Ultimately, the student has paid her dues to get the education, landed the job, and is earning the income now, right? What did the organization actually invest in, the piece of paper on the wall, or the individual who earned that degree? Obviously it is the person. As that saying says "if it is to be, it is up to me." In this life, we determine so much of what happens to us. We must control what we can control.

Along that same line of thinking, controlling what we can control is all well and good, but when discussing working smart, how do we control what we can control? First there must be some sort of understanding of what is meant by the notion of working smart. We have already discussed that efficiency is the basis of working smart, so how then do we control our efficiency with regard to the work we do? We must create systems. Systems are methods that are sequential in nature that allow for the creation of a desired result through implementing effective processes. I like to use analogies and examples and as Stephen Covey wrote when sawing with a dull saw we expend unnecessary energy.

He said "Sharpen the saw". Think about it like this. When a factory is trying to create a more efficient method of creating a product, one of the first things it does is it looks as the process that is used to make the product. In our lives if we are trying to reach a goal, or even accomplish a simpler task, my recommendation is to stop and think about a more efficient method of accomplishing the task exists.

A wise man once told me to "use my resources". This was shared with me while in college, and during a time when I was trying to join a fraternity. I didn't fully understand what this person was telling me. But I have come to understand it through time. While I was trying to research the organization, do my homework and become knowledgeable about the practices that were involved with becoming a member I found I was wasting time. I found that no matter how much I learned about the organization, the things that really mattered involved the things that members of the organization had to share with me. This seems so simplistic, but how many of us struggle with answers to problems or situations as opposed to networking with others who may have the answers? We could be simply picking up the phone and requesting the answer(s).

With all that there is to be said about networking with others, I feel as though a chapter could be devoted to this idea alone. I have not designated a complete chapter to the notion of networking with other individuals, but so many of our predicaments, issues, and life's frustrations could be solved by seeking the counsel of someone with the knowledge to help us resolve these matters.

Finding a mentor who understood personal success and financial and career planning helped to shape my career development. I believe his advice provided a critical element that improved my choices throughout my early college and professional years. I must caution you though. The fact that I recommend seeking advice from others must be accompanied with the disclaimer that only those appropriately qualified to assist in the matters we face should be consulted.

Seeking advice from a medical doctor about your plumbing or asking your auto mechanic about your calculus homework is just silly, right? It does seem silly, but once again, I have witnessed people asking for advice or knowledge about a topic that the person being consulted is simply not qualified to speak about. It seems there is a place for working smart, however hard work can never be replaced. Speaking of work hard, let's talk about how to hustle with a purpose in mind.

Individual destiny is in our hands; we all have the capacity to shape our own futures with the choices of today.

Chapter 9: The Hustle

I once heard Will Smith say "If you stay ready, you ain't gotta get ready". I heard him say this while watching a video on YouTube.com, Will Smith was being interviewed by Tavis Smiley. In the video Mr. Smiley asked Will Smith what was unique about him that has caused him to be so tremendously successful. Will Smith stated, "The only thing that I see that is distinctly different about me is I'm not afraid to die on a tread mill". What he went on further to say is that often times people think it's about another person's ability that makes him superior over others. Will Smith said that he believed that this is not true in many cases. Mr. Smith said that most often if a person has the work ethic to out perform someone with greater talent, then the work ethic will carry that person further than will talent and ability alone.

What does that say about you and me? Are you super talented, gifted, anointed of God?

If so great, if not, if you believe the words of one of the most financially successful African Americans of our generation then all you and I need to concentrate on is work ethic.

I talked about the fact that Mr. Anderson wanted to help me because he saw hustle but I want to take the hustle conversation further. One lesson I learned in my years after college was that the natural energy or talent I had needed to be channeled into a direction that would thrust me towards me end goals. So the natural hustle I had I learned how to channel that hustle and make money at it. I am natural salesman, I have the gift of gab, and I have used that gift to prosper monetarily, but it took taking that hustle and turning it into a skill a craft that people would pay for that ultimately resulted in something tangible that benefited my life. Lifeism #17 *ambition without direction is like being lost without a map!*

Perhaps you are a writer and you love to write but you feel you are not ambitious enough. You hesitate to contact the publisher to whom you were thinking of sending your work. Maybe you are a dancer or a musician and you believe in your craft, but you haven't believed in it enough to demonstrate work to that person you really admire.

Whatever your craft is, what I am saying is that your gift will make room for you, as the Bible declares (see Proverbs 18:16). However, you have to make room for others to see that gift, even if that means making room a hundred times. This chapter is about hustle, but you can't have hustle without persistence. My ultimate point here is simply this, we all must remain steadfast and focused on our dreams, and we must put the work in. Who hasn't heard the saying, "faith without works is dead"? Well, that is biblically based also, see (James 2:17), Again even if you don't believe the Bible, you must respect the laws of the universe. Newton's third law of motion states: "To every action there is always an equal and opposite reaction: or the forces of two bodies on each other are always equal and are directed in opposite directions".

One may argue that a physical law relating to matter has nothing to do with hustle, and I would argue, it absolutely does. Please consider this. If there was a massive vein of oil on a farmer's land that she knew nothing about, but one day was digging a well, and struck a small vein, and a few ounces of oil spilled out. Is she foolish to dig for more oil? Obviously not right, because there is a massive vein of oil, probably worth millions of dollars.

However, what if she didn't know there was a massive vein of oil underground. Is she foolish then? To many people watching what this farmer did on her land for years, she may look foolish, but the day she strikes the main artery of the oil line underground, no one is laughing then. In my opinion, this is an illustration of our lives, I believe we all have the potential to be massively successful; the difference is some will keep hustling and believing while others will just collect social security.

Earlier in these writings I talked about the fact that my mentor took me under his wing because he saw the hustle that I had. This is such an important factor of success. Here is an example of someone who was already successful, had the power to help someone that wasn't on his level, and he chose to help me because he saw I willingly to put in the work. The way I see it working hard and hustling are very similar, but the hustle is that extra effort that extends beyond simply working hard. The hustle I am talking about is sacrificing your summers, or working the shift no one else wants, or even disciplining yourself to the point that once you put the work in you are willingly to prioritize and strategize to reach a goal.

The hustle I speak about is more than working hard, working longer than the next person, or putting more elbow grease into your work. What I am speaking of is a burning desire to succeed that outweighs the fear of failure.

I heard a motivational speaker say that if you want to succeed you must want it more than your next breath, you have to be willing to lose sleep, discipline yourself and focus. The fact of the matter is that most of us don't have people around us making these types of sacrifices. Most people, most average people are not planning on being above average. Most people work a regular job, trying to pay the bills, and at the end of the week have enough to go out and get a movie, go bowling, and have a bag of popcorn. The hustle that I am writing about is a strategic grinding that focuses on your long-term success. We all know that success is different for each of us. However, what I urge you to do is to put a hustle plan together and make your goal large enough that it will require planning. When you decide to hustle there must be a strategic outlook to your grind. As we have already discussed with Lifeism #18, *Ambition without direction is like being lost without a map!*

Maybe you don't want to get a formal education. For you, your goal is to get started in a specific trade or service (such as plumbing, electrical or military service) and be the best in that area of specialization. Then, go get it, go be the best!! I remember being on the phone as an admissions advisor at a large private university speaking with a young man who I believe was in Texas. He was in his late twenties and wanted to complete his degree before he got too old and unmotivated. What I admired about this young man was that he was hustling. He wasn't in school but he was on his grind. Reflecting on this young man's efforts brings to mind a Lifeism #19 *when doing business, never connect with someone that is not busy and already working hard.*

This young man owned his own plumbing company and he had several regular accounts with local restaurants and other businesses. He worked in both residential and commercial areas of plumbing and had his master plumber certification. I remember being so impressed with him because he was focused and had goals and was putting in the work.

He talked about this special device that allowed him to see in the drains, that was different than other telescopic tools many plumbers had. He knew his craft to the point that he could describe it to someone like me and make it easy to understand. Now I am a fairly smart guy, but I am no plumber. Not only did he have his own business he was working a day job, and calling me to discuss getting his degree. He told me that he knew his business was going to be successful. The reason he wanted to get his education was that once the success came he wanted to have a plan and strategy in place to grow the success he would have. I remember that I wasn't able to get him started for whatever reason, but I don't doubt that that young man will complete his degree and grow his business as he told me he would, why? Because he had <u>Hustle</u>!!!!

There is so much to be said about those who know how to put their heads down and grind out their efforts until they achieve the desired results. A wise man once told me, "never go into business with a man that is not busier than you". That doesn't seem too profound, does it? Well, the more I pondered that statement; I found that it is packed with wisdom.

If you or I launch a business with someone who was not already productive, just in the very basic sense of the business deal, we have aligned ourselves with someone that is not active, not trying to move forward. Conversely, simply by connecting with a busy individual, from the onset you at least have momentum, even if the momentum is misguided. If you change the trajectory, the energy will still be there. You must be moving and working towards a goal.

I once heard a businessman put it this way. "In the morning you have to move, so imagine you are a lion or a gazelle. You can choose which one you desire to be. Either way if you want to eat or avoid being eaten, you have to be moving. So when you wake up every morning as the lion or the gazelle, wake up moving."

Don't get this concept misconstrued. Just because you wake up moving doesn't mean you are producing. Which brings me to my next Lifeism, #20 *Activity and Productivity are not one in the same!* I have found this Lifeism to be relevant each and every day of my life. No one ever taught me that I needed to be "producing results" but I understood this idea even as a young man.

Somehow I figured out if I was going to put energy into something, that I needed to see a positive outcome from my efforts. When I was an insurance agent, I was a representative of my company, but I needed to produce results in order to remain a representative of my company. I had an independent contract with the organization I represented so I was self employed but had to meet the standards set forth by the institution that paid me. Ultimately, if I decided not to go into the office, it was my choice but as an entrepreneur you quickly learn that in order to keep your autonomy, the work must be done. Everyday that I went into my office as an insurance agent, I had to discipline myself to set goals and deadlines for the work that needed to be completed. I learned that I couldn't just go into the office and move papers around on my desk, but rather when I went into the office I needed a game plan and I needed to execute that plan. If I did not execute the plan I created my success or failure was on my own shoulders.

If you have difficulty with time management or procrastination, I highly recommend finding an entrepreneur who has had positive financial results. It has been my experience that if you find a professional of this caliber you have just found someone who understands how to cure the problems of being active but not producing results. I am not sure "the hustle" that I have developed can be taught because I have always been the type of person who wanted to make things happen.

However, I am convinced that if you desire to improve personally or professionally, that you need to inspect your daily tasks and determine if you have effectively learned how to decipher the difference between activity and productivity. Once, you have determined that you are not confusing the two, and you are producing, the next question is are you producing the results that you intended to produce?

Again, I am from a small town in Illinois that most people don't know about and I didn't have a plethora of options to choose from regarding finding success. It was simple- either I worked hard and kept to the grind or I failed.

Failure was never an option for me, and it still isn't. I know that I don't always get the results that I desire, and so when that happens, my solution is simple, just keep it moving. There are times when I reflect and change my strategies, but the most important element is that I don't stop working at finding a way to get to the desired outcome. Another part of getting to that desired outcome leads me to another Lifeism, #21 ***Always maximize and utilize your resources.*** Resources are other people, finances, information, skills, time, technology and knowledge among others. I have found that the answer to my problem was within my reach, but the question was whether or not I was willing to stay the course long enough or dig deep enough, or be willing to make the phone call to find the answer.

Notes

Trust God.

Chapter 10: Choosing to Be Different

Who wants to be a copycat in life, I mean seriously? Perhaps some do, but I have found most everyone I have met remembers and likes the original so much more. Take Michael Jordan for example. You can't really get into a discussion about the greatest basketball players of all time with out talking about "Mike". In many basketball fans books, he is the original, he is the man that many compare themselves to. What I see most importantly regarding his character, is that he believes in himself, and he never tried to be someone other than Michael Jordan. This is where some of us miss it; this is where I missed it for many years. I wanted to be good at things, I wanted to be accepted by others and be good at things. I thought would make me happy. Eventually I learned my true inner peace, and inner joy came from making my own path in life.

One of the people that helped me discover this truth was Charlie Stevens. My main man Charlie is a "howlie-boy" ("white boy "in Samoan slang-) from the Big Island of Hawaii.

Charlie came to the mainland United States because he was pursuing and entrepreneurial venture.

I remember meeting him through a buddy in college that invited me to a meeting. I knew about the network marketing "meetings" that took place, and that many think they are scams. So here I am listening about water filters, and skin care, but I was intrigued. I got involved with the Company and made a little money, but I truly benefited from working alongside Charlie. We traveled the country together discussing money, success, our parents and how we are different from them (financially speaking) and we talked about life in general.

It was those "life in general" talks that began to shape my understanding of the importance of being who you are. You may be thinking I am 40 years old; I don't need to learn about myself. Perhaps you have learned this lesson, but maybe not. Maybe you are younger than 40 and you think you have this lesson down pat as well; I will explain how I learned the lesson anyway. One day Charlie picked me up to talk business and eventually we would go into the office, and I knew that.

I had a skullcap on, I was talking a little street lingo, and just trying to act cool. Charlie, called me out on he said "Charles, what are you doing? Are you trying to be someone your not?" He said, "It's obvious to me that you don't fit into this person you are trying to be, this cool guy". "Don't try and follow a pattern that someone else has put forth, instead, create your own path, make your own way". They say there are moments in life, epiphany like moments, when words penetrate your soul and sink in deep. This was one of those moments for me. I understood exactly what he was saying, because he was right.

I haven't talked about my neighborhood much yet so let me enlighten you. I grew up in a medium size town south of Chicago (Population 80,000), where you had to be able to take care of yourself to make it. My town was not like some of the neighborhoods in Chicago that sometimes make the news. I often heard that the Cabrini Green housing projects in Chicago for example, was a very dangerous place, and walking the street could mean life or death on a daily basis.

However, in my community there was regular violence. If you wanted to be able to walk the streets, you couldn't look like a punk, if you did, you most likely would get jumped, beat up, or even worse. So because I grew up in this environment, I had this false personality turned on when I met people. I was trying to be hard, when I didn't want to be hard; I just wanted to be successful. Thanks be to almighty God, Charlie saw this and he called my bluff.

Back to the fact that these words had penetrated the false persona I tried to put on. Because I knew that Charlie was right, I tried to save face and act as though I didn't really get it but deep down, I did get it. Slowly, I started to dress differently and act a bit differently, and Charlie noticed this and began to reward my efforts. I received a promotion within the company, and started to manage a team of representatives. I learned the lesson, if you are yourself, if you put on the real you, your success begins to manifest. Now, don't get confused, I was busting my tail and putting in the work. We all already know that thing called success doesn't just show up at our doorsteps because we change our personality, we have to put in the work as well.

This principle of taking off the masks that have developed as a result of your environment, influence from peers, influence from parents of family, or just not understanding the value of individuality applies to everyone. I believe that no matter your socio economic status, your education level, or where you live you must come to understand that the true inner you, must be tapped into to begin to walk down the path to self-awareness and ultimately enlightenment. Media mogul and successful entrepreneur Russell Simmons supports my claim. In his book *Do You!* He says, "From the beginning of my career, I've always tried to stay true to who I am. I figured it was about time there was a black man who doesn't have to give up his blackness in order to play with the white guys". I notice so many people that walk along side other people that are abusive, that have no direction and that don't attempt to get direction and these people are both spiraling downward away from their true potential.

I recall at phone conversation I had with a young woman I was speaking to when I worked as an admissions advisor at a University. This was a smart young lady, she wanted to go back to school and get her degree, and she had her share of challenges.

She told me about a young child she had, a mother that was supportive and that she had a boyfriend that was in jail. It was not atypical to speak to prospective students over the course of several weeks before they got up the nerve to actually begin classes. This was the case here, I could see that she genuinely wanted a change, but there was something holding her back. One day she got a collect call from her boyfriend and she asked me to let her go, and I told her I would follow back up with her. This young lady was behind on a bill or two and said that when she got her money from doing hair she was going to pay her bills and pay the application fee.

When I called her back she didn't answer for probably a month or two, but one day I got her on the phone. She told me that when her boyfriend called that day that she gave him her money, I don't remember what she said he needed it for, I don't recall it being for his release, but to say the least I felt terrible for her. She said that he didn't work prior to going to jail and that he didn't want to work. Yet, she gave him her money, which was for her bills and her education. That day I found out what was holding her back.

How many of you reading this book know deep within yourself know that something or someone is holding you back. I remember my mother trying to do my laundry when I moved back home briefly after college. I told my mom, "please don't take this the wrong way mom, but please never touch my laundry again. I have to do this on my own". You may be thinking this type of thing doesn't apply to me, I don't need to be told to "choose to be different" I am different. Oh yeah, when was the last time you went to the movies by yourself, sat in the restaurant and ate a meal by yourself, went on a cruise by yourself, did some activity that society says is a group activity, by yourself? You may be able to answer these questions, but this still doesn't mean that you are choosing your own path. Ultimately, what matters is that if this area is something that you need to work on, don't cheat yourself by not being true to the reality of your behaviors.

What I am not saying is that you <u>have</u> to be alone, that you need to alienate people from your life. We need one another, and most of us understand that.

I have not accomplished many of the things I feel were significant without others in my life. However, I accomplished these things with the understanding that it was my path; it was my plan, and my choices that would lead me to these significant accomplishments. It may be terrifying to disconnect from those influences that you know are holding you back.

Think of this way, what if you don't let them or it go? What is the young lady I spoke to about her college education with the boyfriend in jail three or more years ago doing now? If she would have gotten started then and stayed with it, she would either by graduating now or getting ready to do so. This is a simple yet extremely important element to shaping your life for success. If you have to make your own path, and that path is lonely, walk it any way. If you walk alone, and you walk into your true potential there will be a different set, and a different caliber of friends at that level, I am experiencing this as I write these words.

I know about making the choice to be different. It was easy to try and fit in when I was in high school and even college. I remember having so much fun with certain little crews I would hang with in my younger days.

I also remember thinking about where a lot of these people were going, and I started to make choices that I would limit the time I spent with some of these people. In high school my guidance counselor Mrs. Mathews really showed me that is was o.k. to be different. She was an 'old school' AKA. AKA stands for Alpha Kappa Alpha Sorority Inc. She was one of those ladies that you knew cared about you, but didn't take anybody's attitude.

Mrs. Mathews saw my potential and would accept nothing but the best from me. I remember her telling me to watch the time I spent with certain people. She knew I was trying to fit in just to fit in, and she called me out! Calling me out means that she spoke to me about my true behavior, and told me that she understood that I knew better. She set me up with all sorts of opportunities to meet with college representatives, get scholarships and find out about careers. The one thing I remember about the help Mrs. Mathews gave me is that she wouldn't spend time helping me if she saw I was not putting forth the effort she knew I could. Mrs. Mathews, wherever you are, thank you so much I love you dearly for your love and support!

While all of this positive was happening in my life, I saw what ***not*** to do. I will tell you much more about what I saw later. There were people that I hung out with that had the potential I had, but didn't want to be labeled as smart, or didn't want to put in the work to make things happen. Lifesim #22 ***The difference between successful and unsuccessful people is successful people know what to do and DO it!*** As I have said throughout the text this simple principle of watching the mistakes of others and learning from them, truly pays off. At a young age I began to choose the path that was in direct contrast to the path of many around me, but that is the whole point isn't it, I simply saw what ***not*** to Do.

Never underestimate the power of investing in one's self.

Chapter 11: "Faith, Patience, and Trust"

Sometime in January 2009 during my time of devotion with the Lord I heard him speak to me in my spirit (not out loud). Again, many of you reading this book are not Christian, but remember I am. I love you, in a Godly manner, and respect your beliefs please read this and do the same for me. I heard God say within my spirit that I didn't trust him. Being that I have been a Christian and trying to live for God for many years at that point, I was devastated. Within my prayer time I spoke back to God and said "Lord, of course I trust you, I have been a Christian for many years, I have tried to spread your Gospel and be an example for your Kingdom. Again in my spirit I heard God say, "No, you don't *really* and *truly* trust me!" The Lord went on to say, that I would be tested in Faith, and that he would teach me how to have true faith and honestly trust in Him and not in others or in other things.

At some point within three months of God speaking to me in my spirit during devotion, I was praying again, and had another encounter with the Holy Spirit.

The Holy Spirit spoke to me and said, "You will also be tested in trust and patience". I thought, oh great just what I need, more tests. Mentally, I fought the notion of being tested regarding patience because this is one area in which I have a lot of work to do. So, the period of testing began and what a journey it was.

One of the first things I remember about this season was my career situation. I was working for a well-known University in the admissions office. My goal was to be in the admissions office for about 6 months to one year and then move on into the academic area. Well three years later I was still working in that office. Although I had received a promotion a nice salary increase and I was being considered for even higher ranks in the organization, I was unhappy. I was unhappy because I didn't want to just recruit new students I wanted to teach or do something in leadership or administration.

However, I learned some critical lessons during this period of my life. One lesson was the responsibility to put others before myself. As a Christian man I grew up reading and hearing about how the Bible declares that Christ put his disciples, the church and all that he died for before himself, and he served us and even died for our transgressions.

Hearing that was one thing but having to wait, and wait and wait on moving on to a career that I would really enjoy was part of God's plan to build my character. If I am to be a wealthy man one day (and I will be) how does God teach me to serve others? One way is to put me in a career that is all about helping people and focusing on ways on improving their lives, with little to no appreciation for the effort. So for you reading this, what is God doing in your life that seems like it is "not in your plan" that is HIS way of guiding you to becoming a better you.

I want you to take a pen and paper and go to the notes section for this chapter and write about that. If you are an atheist or practice a religion other than Christianity, and you are still reading my book after this many references to God let me say congratulations to you. Congratulations, not because you are allowing me to speak freely, or because you are slowly being converted from atheism. Congratulations, because you are demonstrating the power of keeping an open mind.

Moving on to the trust lessons, and oh how I thoroughly enjoyed being shown what it means to really trust God.

Now in my spirit I argued with God when it came to the issue of trust because I felt I did trust him. I felt that the fact that I was a Christian who read the Bible, believed the bible and openly shared my faith was evidence that I trusted God. Well, there were people in the Bible like Abraham who demonstrated true faith and true trust in God. Abraham was going to slay his only son whom he had waited a lifetime to have to show God that he would trust God. If you don't know about the story of Abraham and his son Isaac see (Genesis chapters 20-23).

So with that said, the level at which one believes they are trusting God is relative. That is to say, because you believe you trust God is one thing, the degree that you actually trust him, is something different altogether. If you don't believe that wait until life puts you into a situation where you have nowhere else to turn, but to a higher power. I am not much of a betting man, but if I were I'd bet your life will lead you there one day.

One of the first things that happened in my life relating to the trusting God issue was I moved to a new state for the first time with no family support. When I say no family support, I am referencing my mother, sisters etc, not my fiancé' and children.

Now let me clarify my mother and father didn't try and stop me from moving away, but they didn't help me financially. Not that I would expect anyone in my family to help me financially, but the fact is I made the move on my own dime (so to speak). These family members didn't have any knowledge about the area we were moving to or really any advice about the transition and the challenges I would face. If you have ever moved to a new place, you understand what I am talking about, if you have lived in one place your whole life you can't appreciate the difficulties I am referring to that you must face.

Once I moved to Florida from Illinois with a good career going I thought all was well. My wife and I were both working, I was making fantastic money, enough to buy mostly all of the things we wanted, life was great. In 2009 my district manager decides to give me a final warning out of the blue, with no prior written or verbal disciplinary actions. To say the least I was shocked. I don't want to go into the whole story but I will tell you this much.

On the day I was given this warning my direct supervisor my sales manager was in the office with both of our district manager the "big boss".

When the final warning from my district manager was handed to me, my supervisor put his head down in disbelief. All three of us were in a meeting sitting around the table. I knew he couldn't show his true emotion, because he had a career to protect, but I knew this person well enough to see he was shocked as well.

I am not the type of person to wait and see what happens, when it comes to the well being of my family. So by the end of that month I wrote my letter of resignation and God had provided a new position with equal pay within that two to three week period. To me, this was a lesson in trusting God, I am not at home, I can't just run to family for support, I am hundreds of miles away and have a family of my own. God provided. Not only did he provide, but he put me on a different career path, one that I really wanted, God is good.

Around this same time my wife and I were in the middle of purchasing a new home in Florida. What was crazy about the situation is how many times the closing date kept getting pushed back. I know home closings can take a long time, but this was ridiculous.

To make a long story short the week were supposed to close on the home finally, the mortgage company was scheduled to call the corporate office of the firm I worked for, to verify my employment. Now I had given my two weeks notice to this organization, but technically I was still employed there. If they had spoken to this senior level officer in human resources in the corporate office the closing would have been canceled. It would have been canceled because the whole mortgage closing was based on the income and work information from this employer, not the place I was going to work for.

      When they called to speak to the senior level officer in the human resources department, they could not locate this person. Now, when I say they couldn't locate this person, the closing representative told my wife and I that no one in the company had any information regarding her whereabouts. What's more is the fact that logically if this person was not available surely there was another human resources employee that could have spoken to the closing representative.

Again, if that would have occurred the deal was off. Somehow, the Lord allowed this person to be missing, and the Mortgage Company didn't speak to anyone else in the corporate office, instead they called my direct supervisor. My director supervisor supported me, as I had done a good job for him, and he verified my employment. This wasn't a lie, technically I was employed with the firm, but I had given notice, he just didn't provide that information, praise God! Lifesism #23 *Trust God.*

I believe faith and trust are two distinct ideas. To me faith is believing that God is real, and that the things he says he can do, he can do them. Let me provide an example of how I perceive faith and trust to differ. Let's say I told you to sit in a chair. I tell you to have a seat and I pull the chair out for you and ask you to have a seat. What do you do? You take a seat and sit down, obviously right? O.k but now let's say I ask you to have a seat in this same chair, but before I ask you to sit down, as I pull the chair out for you, I slip a blind fold over your eyes and spin you around and move you throughout the room. At the same time I move to the other side of the room and tell you to have a seat. What do you do now?

Not so obvious, some people may say oh sure I would trust you and sit down, but if you are honest with yourself, you may hesitate a bit.

This is what I dealt with when I began my journey of several tests of faith, patience and trust. I began to have a deeper understanding of what it means to sincerely have trust in God, not just faith in him. As of the time I am writing this chapter, I have been laid off of my job as I complete my doctorate degree, and have actually experienced an increase in income. More specifically, our family business provides significantly more income than the job I was laid off from.

No matter your faith, even if you don't even believe in God, I still urge you to trust that there is a power that works on your behalf to see you through circumstances, as long as you do your part. Your part will vary based on what you believe your part to be. If you are a religious or spiritual person, perhaps it means paying your tithes and serving others. If you are not a religious person, it could be to work hard, and appreciate what you have been given in your life by consistently having a positive mental outlook.
If you d

o not have a religious belief system, perhaps doing your part means sticking to a plan a strategy that you have to make progress in your life. Either way, if you choose to move towards your destiny, I am confident that the universe desires to support that choice and aligns opportunities set aside for you and you alone.

Consider the quotation by Scottish mountaineer and author W.H. Murray on commitment that I discussed in chapter 8 (see page 68). There is a correlation between trusting God and commitment, in both instances; you have to decide to *give yourself completely* to the idea or action.

Life is God's gift to you, what you do with your life, is your gift to God.

Chapter 12: Bishop Carlton Pearson

Obviously, by now you know that I am a man that lives by faith, and you may wonder how I got this way. Well, one of the reasons, I am the way I am, is that I have always seemed to have great favor with men and with God. It is not something that those who don't believe may be able to understand without some explanation, so let me tell you about one example of this favor that I speak about.

A world renowned Bishop, pastor, author, recording artist, television host, and leader in the Christian faith by the name of Bishop Carlton Pearson, has deeply touched my life. When I was in my twenties my Bishop, Bishop Abe Richardson Jr. was a part of what was known as the AZUSA Fellowship. The AZUSA Fellowship was the epitome of conferences within the African American Christian circle during the 1990's until its demise, sometime within that decade. Today Bishop T.D Jakes' Megafest is as AZUSA was in times past.

It is my understanding that Bishop Carlton Pearson was responsible for giving voice and national recognition to many of the ministers and preachers that many Christians follow today, including Bishop T.D Jakes. As a side note, I do not agree with Bishop Pearson's current biblical views of 'inclusionism' but I honor how Bishop Pearson's spiritual wisdom impacted my life.

I heard that Bishop Pearsons' conference in Tulsa Oklahoma was a huge event, I had never attended the event, I had not known how many people attended at that time, I just heard it was a big deal. I later learned that often times the Oral Robert's University stadium in which the event took place could be filled with between six to ten thousand people and that the overall conference attendance could top 20,000. When my Bishop invited me to travel with him one year to the conference, I was excited to say the least.

Upon arrival to Bishop Pearsons' church Higher Dimensions Bishop Pearson greeted my Bishop and Pastor personally. I thought that was pretty cool. It was obvious this church loved Bishop Pearson; you didn't need to be a genius to feel it in the air.

Once at the conference I started to get a sense of why Bishop Pearson was such a big personality, his charisma was infectious, and he was sincerely loving, which was an endearing quality. He was very well connected as well. I had the privilege of meeting Donnie McClurkin some years prior to AZUSA in Illinois. Pastor Donnie, as many know him, is a well-known singer and pastor. One day at an event leading up to the conference Pastor Donnie was there, and walked up behind me and gave me a hug. I told him I had met him, and he remembered, I thought, "OK, I need to hang out with this Bishop Pearson".

To make a long story short, one evening after the conference the pastors and leaders where invited to an exclusive coffee and tea sort of private meeting with the Bishop. My pastor asked me to escort her. Now, this was a big deal because Bishop Pearson was a very influential person, so as a Pastor to have a chance to speak with him personally it could open doors for you. The Bishop was an advisor to then President George W. Bush, had a national television program, he was someone to know.

During the event, the host announced Bishop Pearson's arrival, and everyone applauded. Before he greeted anyone in the room he walked right up to me and put his arm around me and started talking with me. I have a picture with him that my pastor at the time took, and I look so shell shocked, it is funny to look at it now. When Bishop Pearson started talking with me, it was extremely exciting to say the least. He gave off a good energy; I could just tell he was a kind-hearted man. He began to ask me about my life, and what I wanted to do with my career. All I can say is that this was highly intimidating for me. I didn't know him, and he definitely didn't know some kid from small town Illinois. As I said earlier I have found favor with men throughout my life, and this was certainly an example of that occurring.

Why did he walk over to me? Was it purely just random chance? Perhaps some would say so, but I must say I know better. As he began to talk with me, as he concluded he said these words "No matter what you decide to do, it will be great". I thought nothing of what he said, other than the fact, that I was honored to meet on a personal level someone so many people admire.

After the event, my pastor and I were driving back to the hotel, and we started to chat. She said, "I noticed Bishop was talking with you" "Yea, it was pretty cool" I said. She asked with a very surprised look on her face, what he said to me. I told her what he said, and she looked at me and said, "Do you realize what just happened to you? I said, "No, I don't know". She said "Not only is Bishop Pearson, a popular man, he is God's authority and overseer of this work. When someone in authority speaks over you, in the spirit realm it is similar to a governor or a president pronouncing a promotion over your life in the natural arena. Many would love the opportunity to have him talk with them one on one and he singled you out, you just have received a spiritual blessing from God's chosen man, this is a moment that will change your life forever."

As I walked back to my hotel room, I began to weep, and I couldn't explain why, but I felt the holy spirit minister to me, and tell me that this moment was as special as my pastor had explained. Some things simply cannot be explained.

Do we know how the stars came to be in their place? Or how it is that the distance from the sun is such that we never overheat on earth. Or why you feel a certain feeling when you kiss someone that you truly connect with? This meeting between Bishop Pearson and I occurred sometime in 2001 or 2002 over twelve years ago, and I can truly say that my life has continued to prosper, God doesn't lie.

This was not the only amazing event that occurred while attending Bishop Pearson's AZUSA conference. The meetings were fantastic; they featured well-known ministers from around that country that discussed relevant topics, that spoke to issues and areas that I could relate to. Bishop Pearson called for early Morning Prayer during the conference, and I remembered what my pastor had told me about making sacrifices. She said, "It takes a special sacrifices to get to the depths of God". It didn't mean all that much to me at the time, but I was a Christian. There was a time I didn't commit to God, so now that I had, I wanted to do it to the best of my abilities.

The prayer started at 6:00am, and for me this was a sacrifice, because technically this was my vacation.

I recall waking up around 5:00 am and being groggy, sleepy and every other emotion of tiredness and headed into the auditorium this way. I have never really drunk coffee, but felt like something strong like that was needed.

The prayer began and I will say there was and still is something special about this time of morning. Again, one of those things that is hard to explain, but it felt as though praying was easier, it was as if God was more readily available. I know that God doesn't sleep and that he doesn't need to have less people praying for him to hear me. However, it makes sense that if there is less clutter in the spirit world that he could hear me clearer. The prayer shifted to people just sort of praying on their own as opposed to someone leading from the pulpit. I remember leaning over a chair, and someone tapping me on the shoulder. I stood up and it was Bishop Pearson's spiritual mother.

I don't recall her name; I believe he called her mom, or momma. She leaned over to me and whispered these words, nearly verbatim.

"The lord is pleased with you, and says that if you will stay with the Lord and be made, that God himself will make the enemy give back to you, everything thing that the enemy has stolen from you".

So here it is twice that people that do not know me are telling me things that I have no idea why they are speaking them to me. First of all, as I said they don't know me, and secondly, they are finding me amongst all of the other hundreds or even thousands of people in attendance. This leads me to believe that again, for whatever reason, God has selected me and blessed me among men. I cannot remember all that was happening at the time, but I recall that I had a car repossessed. I also lost a good paying job, a few months prior to when Momma Pearson (as I will call her) had prophesied to me. For those that are neophytes to spiritual lingo, a prophecy or prophetic word is such that someone foretells the future, or explain events that have yet to take place in your life. Also, Momma Pearson, is the name I am using she wasn't Bishop's biological mother.

Sometime after the conference once I returned back to Illinois, I was reflecting on the events that had transpired at the conference.

I remembered that Bishop Abe had told me whenever someone prophesies to you, don't be so excited about the prophecy that you don't write the words down. He explained that you write the words down, to allow the Lord to prove himself. That is to say, once the prophecy comes true, you can look at the date on the prophecy and see that God kept his word. So this is what I did. I have always kept a journal, and I wrote as much of the event in the journal as I could, including the prophetic word, given to me by Momma Pearson.

One day a good while after writing the journal entry I was looking at the journal entry and thinking about how well things had went since writing them. At the time, I was looking at the journal entry I was driving a new luxury car, had a great new business that was going fantastic, and I can't remember if I cried that day, but I am guessing I did. This was a miracle to me because when I got my car repossessed I was crushed. I am not a weak-minded person, I believe in hard work, staying positive and keeping a good attitude. When my car was repossessed I was at an emotional low point because I was doing the things I knew I was supposed to do. I can remember so vividly the days on Green Street on the University of Illinois campus at the bus stop right in front of the Illini Union.

I would wait for the bus there quite often. After my car was taken I would stand there waiting for the bus, watching other people drive their cars. I was in sheer agony, from the pain that I felt. I felt that I let myself down, I felt I let my family down, I felt I let God down, it was a dark time.

To have this journal entry that said that if I stayed with God that he would restore me was something magical. I can't explain how all the good things took place, but they did, and God had kept his word. Now, I am not the bragging type but let me say, that not only did God keep his word he blessed me. Please know I understand God's blessings include more than material possessions. However, I must say that among the luxury car and a successful business were a blessing in my life and other people noticed.

In fact, I spoke to my mother recently and she was telling me how my reputation is still very strong in my hometown, even though I moved away several years ago. I know that I worked hard on being an honest businessman and building rapport with people. However, deep down I know that the word I received prophetically, along with God's favor are the reason that I was walking in victory, Praise Jesus!!!

Notes

Never be afraid to be the only one on a path, every path begins with a leader!

Chapter 13: Mental Toughness

As I watched the 2013 NCAA "March Madness" Men's Basketball tournament games one particular matchup stood out. My schedule at the time of the tournament was fairly hectic as I was at a critical point in writing my dissertation, so I couldn't really relax and enjoy the tournament. However, the sweet 16 game between Louisville (1 seed) and Oregon (12 seed) caused me to reflect on a critical factor of success.

The #2 guard for Louisville Russ Smith was relentless. I have played and watched the game of basketball for many years and I consider myself fairly knowledgeable on the overall way the game should be played. Oregon had a serious opportunity to win the game, although they never led the game they cut a deficit that at it highest point reached 18 points down to 6 points. I read a little about Louisville, who was the #1 seed in the tournament and this 6 points was the closest any opponent had gotten to them in several weeks.

The difference in the game, in my humble opinion, was not the 31 points, 2 rebounds and 3 assists Russ Smith of Louisville had, although dominant. The difference in the game was as Oregon crept closer and closer, Russ Smith (fighting a cold) was defiant and kept finding ways to score and pass for assists. Such must be the case in life if we are to win.

I remember sometime in 2008 or 2009 when I actually had time to watch golf and when Tiger Woods was the #1 golfer in the world. By the way, I would be remiss if I didn't mention just last week he reclaimed the spot of #1 in the world over Rory McIlroy. I recall watching a tournament and during an intermission they played a special on the topic of the "science behind a golfer's mind". The topic may not be exactly accurate, but it was along this line.

Obviously with Tiger woods holding the #1 ranking, the program mostly talked about Tiger's golf game. One of the topics the program discussed is a golfer's heart rate and adrenaline. I may not be getting all of this completely correct, however the basic premise was that when many golfers on tour are under pressure their heart rate rises, but with Tiger it's completely opposite, he relaxes.

So now you have a little better understanding of how someone could be so dominant within his craft, he built a concrete tough mentality. You would have to ask Tiger how he built this mental strength, but regardless of the how, we have to start with the foundation, we now know another ingredient in our success soup (if you will).

Life in so many ways is like sports. In both, you need a good coach, in both you must consistently work on your craft, in both there are winners and losers, in both those that put the work and time in, are often times the ones who win. Ultimately most always in both, those that commit to winning, eventually win. I believe the parallels are even more numerous than what I describe here, but this at least paints the picture. When I watch sports, I watch for heart in the team or individual athletes. I watch for body language, I watch for that determined look and I watch to see who has given up. I cannot tell you how many times, I have predicted who would come out victorious in a game, because I could see that fire that some athletes possess, that fire that burned and propelled them all the way to victory.

This fire, this burning confidence and desire to overcome, I believe it starts in our minds, but it must travel to our hearts.

I attended a conference in 2012 where one of the presenters talked about the neurological research that affects athletes and everyday people alike. According to this presenter, a PhD in psychology, when we are given a directive, if that directive was given emphasizing the negative, our minds focus on the negative, even though the goal of the directive was the opposite. For example, if someone is talking to a child while he is riding his bike and there is a tree near the sidewalk he is riding on. When the child is getting close to the tree you yell out "Don't hit the tree".

What happened to the child? I bet you knew I was going to say, he hit the tree. Why? because the directive was given in the negative. Instead of "don't hit the tree;" if you would have said "stay on the sidewalk" the child focuses on staying on the sidewalk, not avoiding the huge tree. I said huge because often the smallest things to us adults look huge to children. Don't believe me, have you ever visited your grade school years after graduation only to realize, everything looks so small.

Mental toughness obviously begins in our brains, we must learn ways we can focus on the positive and avoid the negative.

I could introduce scientific and neurological research on the psychology of mental toughness, but this book is written to the common winner. Without all of the science and technical knowledge, what it boils down to, is that if we are going to win, we must believe we can win. Not only must we believe we can win, we must believe we deserve to win. I have found that it is often times human nature to simply not have faith and confidence, and a belief system that communicates that we deserve to be successful.

I talk to myself, and I command myself to think positively, and to believe in my abilities. It may sound crazy to some, but I stand in the mirror and tell myself I am a champion, that I am a natural leader, and to hang in there during tough times. I work to convince myself of my own worth, especially when surrounded by negative people or those trying to tear me down. This is just my personal viewpoint but I believe we all doubt ourselves at some point along the journey. This doubt should only be temporary; if we focus on developing confidence in our abilities this doubt will eventually fade.

The doubt will fade because in time, we can look back over our shoulder and see all the accomplishments we have achieved as a result of our mental toughness.

Perhaps, you are asking yourself how does one develop confidence? Well, since the sports reference and analogies are simple ways to present the principles behind mental toughness let's talk basketball once again. Lets imagine a scenario in which you're not very good at basketball and you attempted to take a few shots over the course of a few days with someone who possesses decent basketball ability and you decided to learn to shoot. One way you could be taught is to start shooting near the basket and using the backboard, learning how to shoot a bank shot. Now, some folks reading this book know all there is about basketball, some know a little, and some may not know much at all, so all please bare with me as I try and illustrate confidence being developed.

O.K so now you are shooting the ball off the backboard and the first day you are not very good at it. Over the next day or so you begin to get the hang of it, and by the end of the week you are making nearly every shot you take.

What just happened? Confidence was developed. You began as a novice, and now you have experience and you are making basketball hoops. Such is life. Furthermore, this is what is required if you desire to develop one of the essential ingredients in mental toughness, confidence.

I know there are people that have been beaten down all of their lives. Some of you experienced bullying at school or from the neighborhood kids. Others of you endured mental and emotional abuse from parents of family members, and others of you have been ostracized and have never fit in all of your lives. I know this to be the case because I have spent years developing relationships, working in industry, serving in ministry and just spending time with people. Please be assured that not matter what your history, you are not without the ability to create a much different future, but I highly recommend you engage yourself and learn the principle of mental toughness.

One of the most critical purposes I stress that mental toughness be amongst the skills you obtain is that on the road to your individual place of success you will be tested. I am reminded of the biblical story of Joseph.

For those that don't know the story according to Genesis chapter 37 through chapter 50 Joseph was a seventeen-year-old boy that found higher favor with his father than his brothers because he was born when his father was old. His brother's sold him into slavery and all the while the bible says that God was with Joseph.

The short version of the story is from being sold into slavery Joseph was thrown into prison, falsely accused of sleeping with another man's wife, and lost his position as head of an Egyptian master's house and possessions. Through all of this, Joseph ultimately became second in command of all of Egypt only answering to the Pharaoh. Joseph possessed mental toughness, and many Christians would say he had God's favor and faith in God all the while.

If you respect the law of gravity, respect the law of process

Chapter 14: The Process

Some time back as a young entrepreneur wanting to make my mark in the music business I was fortunate through connections to meet Mr. V. Michael McKay. One summer I planned a trip to Chicago and he made himself available to speak with me regarding music, his career and helping me to move forward with my goals and aspirations. Mr. McKay is a Grammy award winning songwriter, producer, music director and now acquaintance of mine. During my trip "Mike" as he is called invited me to lunch and we spoke about all sort of things including music, family and life in general.

Me being the sort of young man that had major ambition and was full of what I thought was knowledge, I often would challenge what others said. And so was the case during this meeting. Mike and I were talking about his brother. He mentioned that his brother was on the wrong path making bad choices etc. I said "God wants your brother saved, and out of that situation". At that point Mike, sat back in his chair and smiled as I went on with this line of thinking in our conversation.

After listening to my version of the situation, he sat up and calmly said, "I'm sorry to break it you son, but your wrong".

We got into a heated conversation about the fact that God order's people's steps and there is a way God wants our lives to be shaped. Mike said that everything is a process, and just like you got on the right path and weren't making some of the bad choices his brother is making, that his brother will have to endure the process and find that correct path in God's time. I fought what Mike said, and of course disagreed, respectfully of course. I had a great trip and Mike and I became pretty cool. By the way Mike if you read this, I really appreciate the lessons and limited time we shared, God bless you my man!.

So is Mike right? Does his brother need to go through his own process as Mike said or was I right in that there is no excuse for him making all these mistakes and he should be on the right path? Well after much deliberation and life experience I have come to the conclusion that Mike was right that his brother, as do all of us, must go through our own individual processes in life.

Let me explain. Let's just use a hypothetical situation to illustrate my point. Let's say a young woman is in college studying electrical engineering. She wants to get married, have children and have a great career. Let's call her Adrianna.

She is the atypical woman who wants her cake and wants to eat it to, and she is willing to do whatever it takes to "have it all". After college, Adrianna is devastated by an illness that nearly kills her and leaves her infertile, and the man she is dating decides he can't take it and leaves. Now she is a 33-year-old single woman with a career but no family and no way to have children. She is depressed she can't sleep and sometimes has suicidal thoughts.

The day before she decides to end it all she gets two phone calls, one from her doctor and another from her first love in high school. The doctor tells her to come in right away there has just been a breakthrough in her condition and he thinks it will reverse her illness. The ex-boyfriend has been out of a serious relationship for 5 years and has thought about her for years and finally gave in to calling her. At the end of it all she is able to have children and marries the man she was supposed to be with all along.

One day at work Adrianna goes into the bathroom and hears sobbing in the stall and says "hello, is someone there". It is a coworker that has a bottle filled with powerful prescription drugs about to commit suicide. Her coworker has reached the point of taking her life not only because of her illness, but also because of the depression in her life that has resulted from the "hell" within her marriage. Her coworker has the same condition Adrianna had and her doctor doesn't know about the medical breakthrough that reversed Adrianna's condition.

The young woman's doctor doesn't know because the FDA has not approved the treatment in the U.S, as it is only currently available abroad. Adrianna is able to share her story and saves her coworker's life. One word- process. I just this story up, but I made it up with the understanding that many times we go through our processes so we can become stronger. Sometimes our processes are designed to help someone else along the way or for some other reason we won't understand for years down the road. My life and my experiences have taught me that the process is necessary, not only is it the way the systems of the world operates, it is life.

When you stop and think about life and the "circle of life" there are so many things that are processes. A woman that carries a new baby must endure a process, getting an education, learning how to write, learning how to walk; even learning how to talk is a process. Every time you sit at the dinner table and eat that pasta or steak or chicken you are literately eating process. Why are you eating process? Simply put, everything that you are consuming had to go through a process to become consumable.

I am not an agricultural specialist, but we all know that if we are consuming some sort of meat, that animal had to develop as an egg or in its mother's womb, it had to grow to maturity. The meat or product had to be processed and then it became your meal. The process of a steak becoming your dinner took years to produce that meat. Almost anything thing we think about that exists came about as a result of process. As I talked about in Chapter 11 Faith, *Patience and Trust,* it all takes time. I am not the patient type, I like to keep things moving and shaking so this process business is still a challenge for me. However, I respect it, just like I respect the laws of nature.

That brings me to Lifeism #24 ***If you respect the law of gravity, respect the law of process***. The laws of nature such as gravity, lift, causality and various energy related laws have serious consequences. Not respecting gravity and jumping from a skyscraper, most likely means death. The processes we must endure are much the same. I have never read that a law of process exists. However, I am convinced that someone could explain what I am saying, and relay the information in scientific terms. Simply put, if the natural order of things takes time to evolve, if most all changes, if growth and development in nature go through processes so must the things we desire in life.

As I said previously the purpose of this book is to provide you the reader, with examples of what not to do and a new perspective on life and its challenges. Perhaps you have never thought about that fact your frustration regarding your career, family issue, relationship problem, spiritual matter or other difficulty is a result of not embracing your process. You don't have to be a religious person to understand that the world existed before you and I got here, and that the system and law of process was in place before we came.

There were natural laws that were in place and controlled the way the world functions prior to your and mine arrival here. I have found that the sooner I embrace the fact that these laws will be dominant in my life, the better my life will be.

I recall a time when I actually used Facebook, I was reading a post a minister had written that said something along the lines of: Don't be so quick to *get out* of the situation your in, if you do, you may not *get* what you were supposed to *get out* of the learning process within the situation. It is inevitable that we will go through trying times. I have to come to believe during these times there is something to be discovered about ourselves, about the world and about our life's journey and purpose. When I was younger I was fairly poor and had a childhood surrounded by unsafe neighborhoods, racial discrimination, limited economic opportunity and a lack of positive role models. All of these factors shaped my childhood, but how I responded to these challenges shaped my character.

In fact, when I was a college man, or maybe after I graduated college, I had a conversation about character with Dennis, a good guy I knew that worked at the local bank. I sat in his office and we talked about success as black men, and the challenges we faced to move onward and upward as professionals. Our conversation transitioned to personal challenges and how to overcome things we went through. I will never forget, as I talked about a certain issue, and how it was really hard to get through this particular issue. Dennis began to talk about his father, and what his dad taught him about life's challenges. I can't quote him, but the essence of what he said was, *every time there are challenges that seem to overwhelm us, during this time God is trying to shape our character.* Lifeism #25 **keeping the right perspective, during life's challenges, is the first step in moving onward and upward after the storm is over.**

All the days of my life I will never ever forget that conversation. It changed my perspective of how to face the things I was going through. As a Christian I know that my God loves me, so why would my heavenly father put me through something to harm me?

Would I make my own son go through something just to cause him pain? Absolutely not, why? Because I love him entirely too much to purposely cause him harm.

As I said at the onset of this chapter we must go through the processes that life demands of us. I have determined that one way to shape our lives to position of for success as we move forward in life is to seek knowledge and wisdom regarding our challenges and difficulties. Most likely there is some information about you or I are facing from some source we trust will provide us with comfort or a way of the situation.

For example, if a soldier is commissioned to travel off to war if he or she is to advance in skill and understanding of becoming a more skilled soldier, the experience of war is required. Although most civilians wouldn't want anything to do with a battle of war, a soldier that understands his responsibility and his duty will willingly go into a fight. With much prayer, skill and competence that soldier has an opportunity to successful navigate the challenges of war, and on the other side of the experience is a better soldier, such is life.

I once heard the late Dr. Zachary Tims say, "it takes three things to make a diamond, time, heat, and pressure".

We all want to be 'diamonds' but many of us avoid the process that we must endure to attain the brilliance and shine we so desire. I have heard it said that in order for certain types of photographs and X-rays to be 'developed' they must go through the 'dark room'. You probably understand the metaphor, but simply put before the end product there is an uncomfortable middle process.

Bishop TD Jakes further develops this concept of the process in one his sermons. He referred to our mindset when we think of process in reference to our life's journey. He said that many of us don't think about our life in terms of steps we have to go through to reach our desired destinations. According to Bishop Jakes many of us think of steps in a process as a gradual progression and not a gradual inclination. He went on to say that as you stand before a flight of stairs, you normally start at step one before you go to step two, and if you try and skip a step the chances of tripping increases. I credit Bishop Jakes with the concept of a flight of stairs that can be used to illustrate the often difficult processes we must endure, but I have another insight to add to his illustration.

Once you are climbing the flight of steps it becomes more difficult to expend energy the further up the steps you go. Simultaneously, you expend more and more energy as you are getting closest to your destination when it seems it is the most difficult to continue to take just one more step.

Now that I have discussed the importance of understanding the various processes we must endure on our individual journeys I must remind you about endurance. There is a biblical phrase that many use that states, "the race is not given to the swift nor to the strong, but the one that endures to the end". There is also the story of the tortoise and the hair, and how the hair lost to the tortoise because the turtle just wouldn't stop going. Learning to endure through the storming seasons of process is never easy.

From time to time, I find myself thinking negatively, doubting the process, wanting to be through the process, but one thing I never do is complain. The Universe, and the creator reward us for our positive mental attitudes. That is to say, if you can remain positive and stay focused on the end result of what your process will bring you, you will conquer the pain of the often times long lasting process.

Again, it has never been an easy thing for me, and I imagine it won't be for you either, but as it is often said, no pain, no gain!

Your thought life determines your real life.

Chapter 15: The Imaginative Mind

I have always been amazed at the expressions of the paintbrush from the imaginers' mind. I think of great artists, poets, authors, leaders, and humanitarians that have created masterpieces because they let their thoughts run wild. Wouldn't it be a wonderful thing if you and I could dream a dream, bring the dream to reality and then it brings joy to humanity? Think of the late Walter Elias Disney who created an animated mouse and now his legacy and entertainment venues bring joy to multitudes every year. Also, the late Steven Paul Jobs the visionary behind apple computers, cofounder of Pixar animation studios and legendary technology expert. In thinking more historically, after a century of his architectural influence Frank Lloyd Wright is often regarded as the most imaginative architect of all time. Lastly, the recently late humanitarian Nelson Mandela often referred to by his clan name "Madiba". Nelson Mandela imagined a South Africa free from racial divide; he lived as a revolutionary visionary and died a global icon for unabated justice.

The pages of this book could not contain all of the wonderful imaginative minds of men, women, young adults and even children that have influenced the world. The one who possesses an imaginative mind, is the one who dares not only dream of the possibilities outside the voices that say it cannot be done, this individual also creates and discerns the inner voice that transcends the constant barrage of pessimism. Growing up I didn't see many examples of the imaginative mind, on my neighborhood block or at my schools; I found my own imaginative mind through reading, exploring new things, learning about myself, and through God's gift of wisdom.

In thinking of the philosophy I am presenting throughout these writings regarding finding your inner voice and spirit, one could argue it is intuitive that our inner voice has creative and imaginative potential. Why? I'm glad you asked. I believe God created the heavens, the earth and mankind. If the one that creative us was imaginative enough to create all we see, should we not have the same ability? For the less spiritually minded perhaps providing a different perspective would be fruitful.

One could rationally conclude that just as we are logical thinkers we are creative thinkers simultaneously. Why is this the case? Although I am not a neuroscientist there is research that supports the notion that the brains' hemispheres have the ability to allow both logical and creative thought processes (see Pink 2006).

It has been said that, "seeing is believing". The underlying message behind this phrase is that until an individual is able to see something with his or her eyes that there is doubt that that "something" exists. Mr. Steve Jobs' presentation of the tablet to the marketplace comes to mind. To my knowledge no device such as the electronic tablet was available on the market place prior to apple's iPad. I don't know the research or ideas that preceded the actual development of the iPad but the iPad went from a concept in someone's head at apple to a physical tangible product you and I can touch today. My point is that if you and I allow thoughts like 'seeing is believing' we could be missing out on our individual winning ideas such as apple's iPad product. I'd like to respectfully disagree with the notion that 'seeing is believing, and say that "to see it, you must first imagine it".

I recall thinking that about earning my doctoral degree in high school, I remember it well. Although, at that time, I was unsure of myself, I was young, with little to no financial resources, and had few people around me who knew anything at all about achieving academic success beyond high school. Despite all the things that opposed the thought of achieving such a level, I got it done. Today, I know that the result of achieving my degree was in part due to the fact that I was bold enough to imagine myself as Dr. Bridges. So what can you imagine for yourself, are you willing to see yourself in an improved state of being. The change that you seek is yours and yours alone, but in order to get something different you must imagine it and do something differently than you have to this point in your life to achieve it.

What is it about the imagination that is so powerful? I believe that our minds are like mailboxes. That is to say if we allow our thoughts to take us to certain places of imagination, what we think is delivered to us.

Napoleon Hill in his work *Think and Grow Rich* says " truly thoughts are things, and powerful things at that, when they are mixed with definiteness of purpose, persistence, and a burning desire for their translation into riches, or other material objects".

The imagination and thoughts are not quite one in the same. Webster says a thought is the process or act of thinking and the act of carefully thinking about the details of something. Imagination is defined as the ability to form a mental image of something not present to the senses or never before wholly perceived in reality. I am no psychologist but I would dare to say thoughts happen all the time, but imagination takes work. When I think of imagination other words come to mind, brainstorming, inspirations, dreams, visualizations, creativity and ingenuity to name a few.

I have met certain people and when I speak with them I can just tell they have imagination, they have something about them. Its that sense that sees beyond their senses. Have you ever met someone that talked about what they saw in their mind, or dreamt about accomplishing? Do you know people like this that take their imagination and combine it with action?

If you do, you probably have encountered a successful person. The message here is that if you are a creative, resourceful and imaginative person or know someone who is, that is a good thing but these things must be married with hard work, risk taking, and perseverance if results are to be the outcome.

I found that I have the ability to see well into the future. I also seek out things that inspire me. I have always been driven in the area of entrepreneurship and business and I can always imagine something new in that area. There have been numerous times I have stayed at a luxury resort or driven by an expensive car and wandered what the person that owned these things did to come into possession of them. As I have gotten older and matured I have learned that while there is absolutely nothing wrong with tangible and material wealth there is a wealth that is far greater than these things. This wealth is locked up in the secret of giving, family and in loving those that the almighty has place around you.

I have transcended the imaginative realm of business and gaining financial success to now understanding that if I seek to cause others to prosper and seek to do so with truly pure intentions wealth will find me.

Now, let me caution those that think wealth will find you are me while we simply help others. I believe that as we sow seed, financial seed into God's kingdom and obey his principles while simultaneously serving others, we are positioning ourselves for wealth to find us. This wealth is not only a wealth of a warm heart, and a favorable reputation as a giver, but also a tangible financial wealth. As I have made clear throughout my writing, there is no substitute for hard work, God rewards this, and he doesn't drop gold coins from trees.

Rest assured the imaginative mind, can bring tangible wealth in terms of dollars and cents. However, the imaginative mind for me has brought a desire to continually seek new information and to never stop dreaming or seeking to be inspired to do more with my life. There are many people that will leave a legacy that they amassed a great financial fortune.

The question is how much value do we place on that? Is it a not more noble existence to have gained much and to have given much in return? I believe it is a more noble existence to have given just as much if not more than one has received, and that is my message.

If you ball your fist tight, nothing can leave your hands, and at the same time nothing can be put into your hands either. It is my firm belief that if you will begin to seek to be inspired, seek ingenuity and the ability to be creative, ideas and strategies that will enlarge you will emerge. Upon receiving this inspiration, if you will then take action and move out on your inspiration great things are on the horizon for you my friend, great and wondrous things you have not yet experienced, so let you imagination run wild!!

Notes

Ambition without direction is like being lost without a map

Chapter 16: Finding a Way to Win

Find me a rationale, mentally sane person, and I will show you someone that every day of his or her life desires to win. If someone wakes up every morning and desires to fail, I believe there are a few missing "tools in the toolbox". If you and I achieve success, no matter in what area of our lives, we view it as a good thing. We celebrate success, we take photos of success, we strive for achievement, and we all want to win. Yet so often we don't, we fall short of victory and end in defeat.

I don't believe all defeat or failure is a bad thing, I do believe however, that a mindset that is content with failure is a bad thing, a very bad thing. So that is where it starts then, our minds. We must first establish within our selves that winning is what we want. We must then *decide, or choose* to win. We must next believe we can win, and understand that winning is not simple, easy, or a right. Rather it is a mindset, an action, it requires perseverance and is a privilege. After we establish that we want to win and decide to win, we then must have a strategy to win.

Strategies succeed and fail, and when they fail we must have the resiliency to never ever give up!

I believe where so many lose is in the second part of winning, the desire part. If you don't want it, nobody can want it for you. I recently was mentoring and encouraging a young lady to get her GED. She is a single mom that was going from job to job and not having the level of success she desired. So I was relentless in my encouraging her to get her education, this motivation and encouragement, continued for well over a year. My system of encouraging others is simple, I push until I see your true self, your character, simply put, I push until I see if you want it or not.

Ultimately, I watched as I continued to have success after success in my life and this young lady continued to struggle. She told me she was scared and that she couldn't get over her fear. I pushed her to the point where I got in her face and threatened to "jack her up" (not seriously) in my words if she didn't get on the ball. All to no avail. As I prepared to graduate with my doctoral degree months and months after my attempts to motivate her, she still hadn't even taken the exam.

I once heard the late Dr. Zachary Tims say "You can actually want something so bad for someone that you want it more for them, than they do for themselves". Ultimately, this was the case for the young woman I trying to help, she simply didn't want it bad enough. So the question remains, how bad do you want, whatever it is that you want?

I recall my sophomore year in college. I had an excellent freshman year achieving a 3.3 gpa on a 4.0 scale at the University of Illinois. From my perspective, this was a major accomplishment within itself, because I was the first one to go to college in my family. I really didn't know what I was doing I just wanted my education. I mean I *really* wanted it. Well, after my sophomore year, after too many extra curricular activities, and after a horrible academic year, I was in trouble. I was in trouble with my financial aid situation. There was something instituted within my University called SAP. Satisfactory Academic Progress, this meant for the amount of time a student was in school the student must show substantial progress toward the completion of the degree relative to the time enrolled in class.

Needless to say, my progress was not satisfactory. Ultimately, because my progress was not satisfactory, I faced losing my financial aid, and the real possibility of having to leave school loomed over me.

That summer I got really serious about my education. I *decided* that I was going to complete my degree. I left school for about a year, and made a decision that this time away from school, was just that time away. I committed to myself that I would complete my bachelors' degree. I had help, and I would be remiss if I didn't acknowledge one person in particular that helped me during this time, one of my good friends "Bree" Dawson. One day we were talking about college and the fact that I was out for a while. He took me up to his room, and began to give me the big bro speech about completing my degree. He told me that I really wasn't a member of our Fraternity in its truest sense until I got my degree because one of our pillars was "scholarship". He gave me such a verbal whipping until, after that talk I knew not completing my degree was not only not an option, it was an obligation to myself and to my fraternity brothers.

That following fall when I went back to school, I had to see the Dean because of my poor academic progress. Dean Woolfolk was <u>No JOKE!</u> Wherever you are Dean, if you read this or hear about this book, much respect to you sir, you are the Man! Well, what it came down to was me convincing the Dean that I deserved another chance. So I did just that, I did whatever he told me to do and convinced him I was ready to go back to school. He sat me down in his office one day, and this was one for the moments in my life that I will never forget. He told me that if he signed his name on this yellow piece of paper, that he was signing his credibility on my behalf. At that moment I felt that weight of what transpired, and 2 years later I graduated!

I graduated because I wanted it bad enough that I was willing to pay the price to succeed. Perhaps that is another issue altogether, but I decided to complete what I started and took the steps to get it done. Whatever unfinished task or endeavor you have that is awaiting you, I encourage you today, to simply *decide* to complete it, take action, and you *will* get it done!

For many of you, you are self-starters, you are already wired to be go-getters it is just in your blood. For others, motivation is not an intrinsic part of who you are. You are not lethargic but you need a push or a spark to keep things going. Still others of you are not very motivated at all and even if there is a spark that just often doesn't seem enough to keep you moving and shaking. No matter the category that you fall in the most important element of winning for each of you is the desire to win. Some call it resiliency, some call it resourcefulness, others brand it motivation, and still some say that is pure internal drive. If the source of your spark or fire to accomplish a task fades, in order for you to reach your goals you must learn to surround yourself with others who have the things in life you desire. You must have a strong support system of family, friends, professional colleagues, and when your plan fails, and so often our plans fails, you must not quit.

Recently I heard a scholar discussing the neurological science behind resiliency. He discussed both the practical and scientific implications that affect one's level of resiliency.

The talk was very insightful as the speaker mentioned some of the same principles I outline here such as strong support group, and mental toughness. Ultimately, whether it is proven scientifically or just through practical means, if you or I are to achieve our goals we must decide to have goals in the first place and we must focus on the end result. Steven Covey says begin with end in mind, I say through the challenges remember why you got started, and see your self within the desired state.

For example, if you are an athlete training for an event, envision the moment that you cross the finish line or score the winning points. This mental model of success should be at the center of your training and your process towards success. This mentality is importing during those times when it seems there are very few there to encourage you. It is a must when thoughts of quitting dance through your head. By remembering the purpose behind your blood, sweat and tears, you can reignite the fire, and push through adversity. Envision yourself where you desire to be and I assure you this will reinforce why you are working so very hard.

So when all is said and done what does it mean to find a way to win? I believe finding the winning outcome in various situations in our lives consists of several tasks we must complete.
I also have come to understand finding the winning outcomes requires knowing when there is no task left to complete and becoming wise enough to discern times of action and patience. When we fail, and we all do, we must evaluate what we did wrong, we must correct it or find someone that can help us correct it.

Finding a way to win always means admitting when we have not put in the necessary time and effort to achieve a goal. Conversely, when we have put that time and energy forth we must also be patient for the desired outcome. Winning often times takes patience. This is one of the most difficult things I have learned in my life, to become a patient person. I am a go-getter, I am a mover and shaker and I wake up daily seeking a way to accomplish my goals. However, I have learned that there comes a point that I have done all I can do, and I must wait until things fall in place or until I have learned to make the necessary adjustments.

I have often said that from a Christian perspective one of the most difficult things to do is be diligent and hard working and wait on God to move on our behalf simultaneously. Although it is difficult this is what is required in many situations. This is required whether you have spiritual beliefs or not. If you were to reflect I am convinced you could recall a point in your life that no matter the efforts you exerted things just didn't come together the way you planned, when you planned them to. At times, you have to move out and make things happen and at times you have to patiently allow the universe to bend in your favor, those that understand the difference are those that will find a way to win!

Attitude determines our perspective, and our level of elevation or deterioration

Chapter 17: What *Not* To Do

There are far too many lessons that I have learned to try and share each one here. However, I am convinced there were some things that I watched others do, that were problematic and can be used to illustrate what *not* to do. One of the first things to avoid is procrastination. I remember listening to conversations as a young man in high school and college from my peers about how they were going to put college off for a while and go to work first. I know many of those people never completed their education.

I could not begin to count the number of times I am either having a conversation with someone, or overhear a conversation someone is having about something a person either wants to do, wants to stop doing or has been trying to complete. NIKE and their intelligent marketing people have told us all to "Just Do IT", and they have gotten it right. So much can transpire as a result of actually sitting down and putting in the work. One of the beautiful things about life and especially life in America is we have the ability to *choose* what 'the work' will be.

It sounds so simplistic and so easy to do, but for so many of us, we don't just do it. For the aspiring filmmaker that wants to make a film, going to school and studying film is great, but actually taking out a camera and recording a film is where the *real* education begins. The person who wants to write a novel, and has scribbled notes here and there, will not know the exuberance of actually writing the novel until those notes are put together into a coherent piece of writing with a solid theme, setting, plot etc. The individual who desires to act, and entertain others that lives in a place other than L.A or New York City that decides enough is enough and moves to one the places the real opportunities are is now at least putting their dream to the test. Procrastination is a silent killer, it is a dream stealer, and it is something we must all either focus on overcoming or consistently avoid.

Many of use social media and I think social media in its place can be a positive tool for connection and professional networking. However there are several statistical references that have been published regarding the number of hours the average American spends watching television or on the internet.

One thing I have noticed so many people do is talk about the problem. We all know that watching too much television is bad, but how many people are actually changing their habits, and cutting down the number of hours in front of the tube or online? Ultimately, the time we waste not developing ourselves, cultivating our crafts or learning new things is time we will never get back. Stop procrastinating. Begin today. Who knows how much time we each have in this life, every single day matters, and we must make it count. If you want to write a book for example, and you wrote 3 pages a day in 30 days the book is 90 pages and in 2 months its 180 pages. Executing this example takes more than avoiding procrastination; discipline, desire, and consistency among other things are also involved. However, nothing happens if you don't write the first page.

One of the most important principles I took away from the book, *Think and Grow Rich* by Napoleon Hill is the power of positive thinking and the resulting decisions. Obviously from looking at the title of this book it is apparent the information has something to do with one's thinking.

In addition, it is rationale to understand that when a person thinks positively, that the positive thoughts have power, and can help move the universe around an individual. Just as this principle of watching your thoughts seems intuitive and simplistic, I have found many of the things that allow us to grow and flourish are simplistic principles. The difference is that successful people are the one's who actually implement them. Just as I stated in lifesim #27 *the difference between successful and unsuccessful people, is that successful people know what must be done, and they **DO** it.*

The bible says in Proverbs 23:7 "For as he thinketh in his heart, so is he". In other words *your thought life produces your real life* (Lifeism #28)*.* If someone desires to be a successful journalist they must think about journalism and perform the necessary actions to become the journalist that they so desire. If you or I desire to be a well-known psychologist, the same applies and the principle can be set into motion with any of our desires, not only with a career choice. The problem for so many of us is that although we know the steps we should talk or the thoughts we should think we don't do it. There are countless reasons why, but again, the focus is not the problem but rather the solution.

Ultimately, the solution comes down to the commitment that is executed after the decision is made. In other words, once we decide to move in a direction and we commit to that direction, we must not be deterred to continue in that direction until we reach our destination.

Yet another area that must be addressed to achieve success over circumstance is obtaining patience or avoiding hastiness. Since the essence of chapter is what not to do, let us first discuss avoiding hastiness. I recall a business venture I decided to participate in within the entertainment business. I did my due diligence and secured the details in writing and sought the counsel of an attorney. However, in any deal, no piece of paper that says someone will do something is stronger than the person's willingness and ability to execute the action they commit to on that said piece of paper. So with the other parties' signature in hand I invested a undisclosed amount for studio time, among other items to move forward with my recording and producing career. Due to the fact that I did not take my time and research with whom I was getting involved I lost money.

I met another producer after the money had exchanged hands that said, if I would have talked to you, I could have told you this certain individual was the wrong one to do business with.

I read recently that some business professionals don't like the phrase "at the end of the day" the article stated because it is an overused cliché' it should be avoided in business discussion. Regardless of their opinion, at the end of the day, this was a bad deal. Whether it is a bad phrase to use or not, once the dust settled, I made the mistake of not taking my time and researching adequately and it cost me, in the thousands of dollars. Most likely this is money that I will never get back again.

Let's take it a bit further. How about finding a mate to share your life with. This is one of the most important decisions anyone can make. This is a decision that if made correctly can benefit you time and time again. Conversely, this is a decision that if made incorrectly, and hastily can cause years of agony and pain.

I have been blessed with a wonderful wife that continues to shed new light on the meaning of a blessing to me. However, I have seen so many and heard of so many people that are stuck in relationships that they want out of.

I spoke about the challenges I endured as God took me through the tests of faith, patience and trust. Is it no wonder why patience was in the mix of these areas I was to be tested on, we must just understand, God knows. If you don't believe God knows, I respect that, but it still doesn't negate the fact that utilizing patience correctly can aid us in making the right choices, and in avoiding making the wrong ones.

In order to achieve a certain level of success, it is my opinion that bad relationships must be avoided. What defines a bad relationship, what is the criteria and scope in which we can define a bad relationship? Well, in my view relationships that affect our lives are in three specific areas, personal, professional, and family. Now some may say, we don't choose our family and we just have to deal with the family relationship area. I believe this is true, to an extent. Most rationale individuals love their family members and want the best for their loved ones. Simultaneously, the same rational people understand within the family is often time where some of the most toxic of all relationships exist.

I don't believe in disconnecting altogether with a family member. I do believe in changing the context of a relationship no matter they dimension the relationship exists.

Let's use another hypothetical situation; this way my family can't accuse me of talking about them. Let's say the youngest daughter in a middle-income family has three siblings and is closest to her brother just above her in age. This brother has been in her life as a close friend, supporter, and even a mentor in some respects for years. As the two siblings reach their mid 30s things begin to change. The sister get's married, settles down with children and get's a career moving forward. While her brother starts making bad choices, quits his job and eventually begins abusing drugs. Now the sister loves and adores her brother but one day she notices $150 missing from her wallet and the only person in her house the day before was her brother. She lets it slide, by eventually, finds drug paraphernalia accidently left in a trashcan that one of her children finds. Now, this is when the sister has to make a decision as to how her *relationship* with her brother will be defined in the future.

She still loves her brother but how she communicates and deals with him, must be redefined because the safety and well being of her new family is now at stake.

Just as it is essential to avoid bad relationships, either personally, in our families or professionally, it is just as critical to develop purposeful and fruitful relationships in all of these areas. Why is relationship building so important, and what does it provide us? Just as I discussed in chapter six there are several types of people: adders, subtractors, multipliers and dividers. If we are going to reach our full potential we need others around us to aid us, to encourage us, to pick us up when we fall, and to correct us when we are wrong.

I was watching the Tavis Smiley talk show recently and his guest was Diana Nyad, a 64-year-old swimmer. According to CNN.com, Ms. Nyad had tried four times unsuccessfully to complete the 103-mile swim from Cuba to Florida through shark-infested waters, prior to her recent fifth attempt. During the interview Diana Nyad talked about her team of divers, trainers, shark specialists and others that protected, trained and helped her successfully complete the 53-hour swim at age 64.

She said that it was because of all of the people that worked with her that allowed her to compete at such a high level and be successful.

Ms. Nyad described a period of her swim where she felt extremely exhausted. She said she had swum all night with a protective mask on to protect her from jellyfish stings and this mask was hard to breath through. On her second night in the water after about 35 or so hours in the water and after having to tread water for over 80 minutes because of a storm in the pitch black of the night Diana started to talk with her trainer.

Ms. Nyad told her trainer she was cold because she had been treading water and not swimming, she was hallucinating due to exhaustion, and thought if she could start swimming perhaps she could get her "clarity back again". Her trainer noticed how exhausted she was and pointed to some light in the distance. Ms. Nyad thought it was sunlight but it was actually light from the Florida coast, she was almost to the finish line. She said because her trainer was able to spark her spirit and inspire her to keep going. Ms Nyad explained that somehow she had the most energy she had felt throughout the entire swim at the same time that she felt the most exhausted.

What is the message to you and I? We need healthy relationships and people around us who add to us, and we can certainly live without those that subtract from our lives.

As much as I respect one's right to be an individual, to make their own choices, and to decide what to believe in and what not to believe in I must speak on spirituality. I feel I must do this not out of some religious conviction or obligation. I must speak on spirituality because I believe deeply in my Lord and Savior Christ Jesus and how his love has impacted my life. As I have said throughout this book I am not writing about my spiritual belief because I believe it will magically transform you. I know that I found Jesus not because my parents raised me in a Christian church but because I had an encounter with him personally.

Therefore, if I am to properly outline what not to do, one item on the list of things not to do is to neglect the 'nudgings' of the Spirit. I stated in the preface that some might call this intuition, insight or just a plain old gut feeling, I believe that many times it is the nudging of the Spirit. I am referring to the Holy Spirit that the bible speaks of; perhaps you don't believe in the Holy Spirit then let's just call it the Spirit.

More specifically, I am referring to the times, when you feel impressed deeply about something, or you have a dream or a thought that just keeps coming up in your mind and heart. This is often times the Spirit. In my life it is a daily connection that I seek to experience. For years it was not this way, I didn't understand the ways of the Spirit and had to learn, because even as a young boy the Spirit was always dealing with me and speaking to me.

Let's be clear, the Spirit is not something that is out of a horror film or a spirit that causes schizophrenic delusions. I am not saying listen to the 'voice' that says to do evil, that is another spirit and perhaps I will address that in another book. Please don't use this information as an excuse to do mischief, and say Dr. Bridges said to 'listen to the spirit'. I am speaking to the rationale, sane and competent person that wants to improve his or her life and maybe even help someone else along the way to their own personal refinement. It is unfortunate that I must address this subject in this manner, but experience has taught me some people want to do destructive things no matter what, and they also often times want a way to justify what they knew was wrong to begin with.

Getting back to the point, I once heard, "Our minds are like parachutes, they only work is when they are open".

If you would consider believing that the gut feelings you have from time to time are more than just gut feelings also consider that this 'voice' is leading you with love and wants to help. If you embrace this truth you will discover a new avenue of perpetual triumphs. The 'wins' in life make life that much more enjoyable. Simultaneously, we must endure the loses that teach us valuable lessons we must adhere to. All in all life is a beautiful experience, and remember we all can experience this beauty in a richer, deeper and more meaningful way if we can watch others and *see* what **not** to do!

25 'Lifeisms'
(In no specific order)

---

1. The faster you mentally determine you are unhappy with your current circumstance, the more time you have to change it.

2. Information without application is like a building without a roof, incomplete!

3. Remember having a good reputation is worth more, than having money in the bank.

4. Success principles don't change but we must.

5. Every person's destiny is in their own hands. We all have the capacity to shape our own futures with the choices of today.

6. **Attitude determines our perspective, and our level of elevation or deterioration.**

7. Once you are able to, give back, in anyway you can, no matter how large or how small.

8. Find someone in life who has what you want, do what they do, and you will get what they have.

9. The moment you begin to understand that the world doesn't evolve around you're your perspective is prepared for success.

10. Life is God's gift to you, what you do with your life, is your gift to God.

11. Never try and escape the required effort necessary to build an income generating system.

12. Consistently seek ways to have multiple streams of income and passive or residual income.

13. Ambition without direction is like being lost without a map.

14. Trust God.

15. If you respect the law of gravity, respect the law of process.

16. What holds you back today looks insignificant tomorrow once you've conquered the fear to start.

17. Fear is **F**alse **E**vidence **A**ppearing **R**eal.

18. Opportunities are not missed; they are passed to the person paying attention.

19. Often when we see success in others, we are not jealous of their success, but frustrated that we have not achieved the same results.

20. No matter when tomorrow is, tomorrow holds within it the ability to wipe away all the mistakes of yesterday

21. One four-letter word is always appropriate: WORK.

22. Never underestimate the power of investing in one's self.

23. Never be afraid to be the only one on a path, every path begins with a leader.

24. Your thought life determines your real life.

25. The difference between successful and unsuccessful people, is that successful people know what must be done, and they ***DO*** it.

References

Bar Mitzvah: Entering Adulthood, Lifecycles retrieved online from : http://www.chabad.org/library/article_cdo/aid/1912609/jewish/Bar-Mitzvah-101.htm

Boyle Richard (2000). The three princess of serendip. Retrieved from: http://livingheritage.org/three_princes-2.htm

Chironna, Mark J. (2013). References to various messages and sermons.

Covey, Stephen (2004) Seven habits of highly effective people.

Hill, Napoleon. (1960). Think and Grow Rich. Greenwich Conn. Fawcett Crest.

Jakes, T.D. (2013). References to various messages and sermons.

Murray, W.H. (2013). Boldness and commitment quotation. Retrieved online from the following location: http://blog.gaiam.com/quotes/authors/wh-murray/43217

Newton, I. (2013). Sir Isaac Newton's Laws of Motion. Retrieved online from the following location: http://www.grc.nasa.gov/WWW/k-12/airplane/newton.html.

Northwestern University *Propulsion* retrieved online from the following location: http://www.qrg.northwestern.edu/projects/vss/docs/propulsion/2-every-action-has-an-equal-and-opposite.html

Pink, D. (2006). A Whole new mind: Why right brainers will rule the future. New York, NY. Penguin.

The Holy Bible (King James Version).

Thoreau, Henry David. (2013). Henry David Thoreau, Quotes. Retrieved from http://www.goodreads.com/author/quotes/10264.Henry David_Thoreau

CNN.com (2013). Information on swimmer Diana Nyad. Retrieved online from the following location: http://www.cnn.com/2013/09/02/world/americas/diana-nyad-cuba-florida-swim/

Simmons, Russell. (2007). Do *YOU.* 12 Laws to access the power in *you* to achieve happiness and success. Gotham Books.

Tims, Zachary (2012). References to various messages and sermons.

Back Cover (Extended Version)

Just as there are laws that govern the physical space we occupy on earth such as gravity and lift, there are success laws that control our ascension or dissension, our elevation or our demise. The Universe is unforgiving. Whether we know that certain principles are controlling our life outcomes or not, the results are determined by the application of these laws or the lack thereof. In this book Dr. Bridges unveils a glimpse into his life and how seeing the mistakes of others and avoiding these mistakes is a success principle. Dr. Bridges also outlines personal development tools and skills that if properly executed can help to move you towards a more fruitful and meaningful life.

Have you ever followed the flow of traffic and ended up in a traffic jam? Have you ever used the same door everyone else is using to enter a busy building only to find the line or group of people impeded your progress? Have you ever followed a leader that you felt wasn't doing things correctly only to see you were right?

What if in each of these scenarios you would have chosen a different path, could you have ended up with a difference result? Absolutely you could have. In this book you will find success principles and examples that you may not have ever seen before, because you like so many were looking in the same direction as everyone else. Many times to find our purpose and reach our goals we must look at others and see what NOT to do!

About the Author

Dr. Charles W. Bridges III is a postdoctoral emerging scholar with several years' experience working in higher education. He is a father of three and is married to his lovely wife Nicole. Dr. Bridges was recently appointed as an adjunct professor with nationally recognized Aspen Award winning Valencia College in Orlando, FL. He was also recently an invited guest research presenter at Nova Southeastern University's global conference of leadership, research and learning. Additionally, he is compiling research data for his first academic textbook outlining the latest research on organizational culture in learning organizations. I Saw What *Not* to Do is his first book, it was written to benefit humanity and to aid those on a quest to accomplish the extraordinary.

www.ingramcontent.com/pod-product-compliance
Lightning Source LLC
Chambersburg PA
CBHW070607300426
44113CB00010B/1446